THE REAL WAY TO MAKE MONEY ONLINE

HOW TO SELL ON AMAZON & MORE FOR
BEGINNERS & ADVANCED. MAKE MONEY FROM
HOME & CREATE A PASSIVE INCOME. 9 LEGIT WAYS
TO MAKE MONEY & QUIT YOUR JOB

KEVIN MAGUIRE

KBM PUBLISHING

ISBN: 978-1-950550-08-1

❀ Created with Vellum

INTRODUCTION

A few years ago, I was attending a webinar and was fascinated by the bullshit the speaker was spewing. At this point in my online money-making dream, I was already weary of webinars and avoided them for the most part. But I'd trusted this guy, and he was making sense. When he told me he'd give me 3,000 buyers for my email list, I was sold and broke out my debit card.

I should have known you can't just give people's email addresses away. I did know, but by this time, I was lost in the sales pitch. He was good, and he had me. He made a lot of promises that night, and some of them he kept. He was never going to "give" me 3,000 buyers for my email list, however. He was going to train us on how to create info products to sell on JV Zoo and Warrior+. His partner was the man for that part of the training. We rarely saw him, and he eventually ran with his half of the money before finishing the job.

This first man, I'll call him Joshua, was to teach us the sales part. He is a great salesman and will tell you, "Call me, but if you spend more than five minutes on the phone with me, I've sold you something." He wasn't kidding. He's that good. He taught some copyrighting but not what I would consider worth the money I gave him and his absentee partner. I contacted PayPal and got my money back. It's not something I often do, but those two took us for a ride. Most people, myself included, never got a product on either JV Zoo or Warrior+.

That was a turning point for me. I had been trying everything to make money online, and nothing was working. I wasn't making money; I was losing it. A lot of it. I was an internet marketer's dream, buying everything on JV Zoo and Warrior+. I'd wait anxiously for the next email telling me how I could make $1,748.64 in the next 24 hours, all at the push of a button. I lost a lot more than that figuring out it was all a lie. Maybe you've been there too? I hope you didn't waste as much money as I did.

I was lucky enough to start following a few of the good guys in the business; they're rare. Almost everyone who says you can make a fortune online is selling you a scam. Once you realize that, you'll start saving a ton of money – and you won't have to buy car insurance to do it. One of the guys I started following is Arun Chandran. He's a funny guy who tells it like it is. He is known to rub people the wrong way with his humor, but consider it a test to see if you're serious about making money. He won't sell you garbage and has blocked most other marketers for doing so.

Fun fact: it was one of Arun's PLR products that made me my first online dollars.

The other guy is Adam Payne, and he can go on a serious, fun-filled rant about internet marketers. Adam forbids us from discussing the particulars of his rants, but if you join his *Beers with Adam* Facebook group, you'll get a first-hand look at what I mean. It's not a coincidence that Arun and Adam are friends. They aren't the only two good-guys, but they're the first two I followed that started getting this message through my head: **Most online**

money-making opportunities are scams. I was hard-headed though. It took a while for me to get it. The experience with "Joshua" finally brought that point home.

Internet marketing is rife with scam artists, so here are some other names you can trust: Steve Chase, Andie Brocklehurst, Liz Cheney, and Tiffany Lambert. There are a few more possibilities, but I haven't seen enough of them yet. I'd love to be able to tell you the nastiest of the bad ones by name, but lawyers say that's a bad idea. Furthermore, this book isn't about Internet marketing. This book discusses better ways for you to make those online dollars... with fewer scam artists.

At the same time I was learning not to trust internet marketers, I'd been watching a lot of videos about self-publishing. There is a lot you can do in the self-publishing arena that doesn't involve writing your own books. I was intrigued, but I also knew I had stories in me. More on that later. This is when I started writing books. I'd done the article writing thing and made my pennies there... come to think of it, one of those places still owes me some pennies. I should check into that.

Writing is what changed my life, but don't worry, there's more to this book than writing, I promise. Don't worry if you can't write, however. You can still make a lot of money on Amazon without writing or holding any inventory. Most of it can be done for free or very little cost. But everything started with writing for me. I branched off from there into the print on demand (POD) world.

In this book, you are going to discover a variety of ways to make money online. None of them will be surveys, transcribing videos or medical papers, writing papers for lazy students, writing SEO articles. There will be no arbitrage, selling of domain names, or creating junk info-products to sell on JV Zoo or Warrior+. No, no, no. What I'm teaching are bona fide opportunities from credible companies. Most of it you can start with no money. The first two of those are in chapter 1.

You also aren't going to see photos of me on a tropical beach and a foo-foo drink with an umbrella; you won't see me with a Ferrari or a mansion I don't own. Those are all photos the scammers use to make you think they've made millions. I'm not even promising you'll make millions. I wish I could, but I haven't made a single million yet, so there's that. I will say if you *take action* on what I show you, you'll make money. *How much* is up to you.

*Special note: not all products on JV Zoo and Warrior+ are garbage, only about 98% are. A lot of honest marketers have moved their products elsewhere, but some remain. Payment processors are getting fed up with the return rates there too. But that's another topic.

> *"To get rich, you have to be making money while you're asleep."* -David
> Bailey

Passive income. We all want it; some of us earn it, and you can too. But what is it, really? Apparently, some people think it means you make money while doing nothing or going on vacation. In a way, that is true. But it's not true.

For a passive income, you do the work once and get paid over and over again. Most people only get paid once for the work they do. I earn a passive income by working every day, except December. I take December off; also, half of January and a few weeks in summer. If you love my vacation plan, pay attention to the chapters ahead.

You cannot earn a passive income by sitting on your couch all day watching Netflix. It takes work. It's not 'moving bags of cement that got rained on for 12 hours work,' but it's work. I did that once… once.

You will have to work on your business every day at the start. I still do most the time but will take a weekend off here and there. I have my seven-year-old daughter to think of too. She loves to play with poppa.

But yes, you will be able to make money while you sleep, play, and go on vacation… after you put in the work. Then you must keep putting in the work until you're making the kind of money you're comfortable with. Then you can slow down. I haven't reached that point and don't know many who have.

You bought this book to make money from home and earn a passive income. I will show you the way and prod you to take action. The rest is up to you. It sure beats moving cement.

CHAPTER 1: TURNING PHOTOSHOP, DESIGNER, INDESIGN, AND GIMP INTO CASH

*M*erch

*Special note: Merch only applies to the United States, Canada, United Kingdom, and Australia. If you're outside these countries, hopefully Merch will get to you soon. Until then, skip to the next section in this chapter, Ignite.

This is going to be a short chapter. I debated even calling it a chapter but the "yes" side won out. This is to get you on the waiting lists while you learn about everything else.

If you've peeked at the table of contents, you might have noticed I start with an opportunity and then move to Keywords and Software before *returning* to money-making opportunities. Good. I'm glad you're paying attention; you're going to kick ass at this. There is a reason I did this, and it's because...

You need to take action on these immediately!

Not tomorrow or the next day. Not next week. Today. Now. Or as soon as you read what to do.

Ok, the first thing you need to do is apply for a Merch by Amazon account by going to merch.amazon.com and completing the form. (Now, go and do it! Then come back.) There is no telling how long you'll have to wait for an answer and acceptance is not guaranteed. I know a lot of people who have been rejected, some multiple times. But they keep trying because the opportunity is that good.

I can tell you I waited a year to get accepted. Sending them reminder emails won't help your cause. I also know people who got in after two weeks – right after I was accepted. That seems to be the norm today, but I can't guarantee that's how long it will take.

Nobody can figure out why some people get rejected. It helps to have a website, but lots of people without websites get accepted. The website should be selling t-shirts. Amazon wants people who can *sell* above all else. Some people say designers are rejected a lot. So, if you're an artist, **do not mention it**. Needless to say, if your website is all about being an artist, don't list your website on the application. I know, it doesn't make sense to anyone else either. I'd think Amazon would prefer to have artists designing t-shirts, pop sockets, and whatever they give us next.

If you're rejected, sign up again but use a different email address and change some of your answers. If you listed a website before, don't this time. Make it different and hope for the best. All the trouble is worth it.

I'll discuss the particulars of Merch and Ignite in their dedicated chapters.

Ignite

This one says it's only open to US residents, but people from other countries are being accepted. Ignite is a new program Amazon started a few weeks ago (as of this writing.) I signed up and was accepted after two weeks. Simply go to ignite.amazon.com and fill out the simple forms. One of the questions asks how many designs you will upload. Put a big number. My answer was, "As many as you let me." Then wait. (Go now, don't wait!) I know some people on a few Ignite Facebook groups have waited three weeks so far. There really isn't much information because it's so new. That's why the Ignite chapter is last. It will give me a few weeks to sort things out. I do have my first package uploaded and waiting for approval, however.

To get an idea of what Ignite is about, check out Teachers Pay Teachers. It's the same thing, except it's Amazon. You're creating educational products for K-12. Getting in at the start is an amazing opportunity. This book will be published in plenty of time to jump in at the start. I see lots of opportunity here!

While you're waiting for Ignite, you can make a few products and upload them to Teachers Pay Teachers. You can put the same products on each site, and why not? There will be more eyes on your products and more sales.

These aren't the only ways to make money with designs. There is more in Chapter 10.

Chapter 1 Exercises

1. If you haven't already, go sign up for Merch. merch.amazon.com
2. If you haven't already, go sign up for Ignite. ignite.amazon.com

If you did them already, awesome. You're ahead of the game!

CHAPTER 2 KEYWORDS

Researching and selecting keywords can be an arduous task. But, don't bottleneck your book production process on keywords alone. Keywords only help for discovering your book, not selling it. Get good on your book cover design, book description and writing a stellar manuscript to sell more books.

Dale L Roberts - Free course: kevinbarrymaguire.com/Dales-Startup

---

Keywords are going to make or break your business. Dictionary.com defines "keyword" as: *a word used to classify or organize digital content, or to facilitate an online search for information.*

In this chapter, I'll be using keywords for books as my examples. The same principals can be used for everything else, so don't skip this if you think you aren't going to do anything with books, especially when you read how easy it is to make low and no content books. Easy money is good money!

It's that last part we're concerned with. When you type something into Google or the Amazon search bar (Or DuckDuckGo, Yahoo, etc.) you're typing in a keyword. A keyword can be more than one word and phrases are "longtail keywords." (Some people also call longtail keywords a "keyword phrase." That works too.) So, if I'm on Amazon, and I type "prepper fiction" into the search bar, I'll get a list of books to look at, especially if I clicked the dropdown box and chose "Kindle" or "Books."

When that search finished, I'd have post-apocalyptic fiction that deals with EMP attacks, nuclear attacks, financial breakdowns, viral, etc. There are many ways the world as we know it can end! Maybe I'm not interested in EMP attacks, so I type in "post-apocalyptic fiction nuclear biological financial." That will return more results I'm interested in. "Post-apocalyptic fiction" is a keyword. But "post-apocalyptic fiction nuclear biological financial" is a longtail keyword.

Now, say I'm only interested in nuclear attacks. My search would look something like this: post-apocalyptic nuclear attack. That's another longtail keyword, but it is super niched down. Those are the keywords you want to concentrate on for your businesses. Whether you're designing t-shirts, pop sockets, writing books, publishing books (there's a difference we'll discuss later,) or anything else to do with online commerce, you want to be niched down as far as possible to get the customers you want and need.

Little guys like us can't upload a t-shirt with a keyword of "cats" and expect to be seen. No, we're buried by the big names and their advertising dollars and name recognition. They have followings, and the search engines love them. We must earn that love, and that starts with niching down. When you have your longtail keyword, then you add in the shorter keywords. As you rank for the longtail keyword, your rank for the main keyword will rise with it, just not as fast.

Sticking with post-apocalyptic fiction (and not using a search engine, just out of my head here) I'll walk you through it. We'll get to a real search later in this chapter. My current post-apocalyptic fiction series, *Aftermath of Disaster*, deals with dirty bombs, radiation. That's the first attack, anyway. But maybe my next series will be nuclear bombs, so I'd have to come up with new keywords to list on Amazon.

I would do my search on Amazon.com because that's where most of the books will be sold. At Amazon, I'd click the drop-down box and change it from "all" to "Kindle Store" and start typing "post-apocalyptic" into the search bar. Amazon wants you to find what you're looking for, so they'll offer suggestions. *Pay attention to those.* Those phrases are what people are typing into the search bar. The higher on the list, the more people are searching that phrase.

Those are all keywords, but not all of them will work for you. Ignore the ones that don't fit what you're selling. It will only confuse the algorithm, and you won't be put in the right search results, resulting in zero to few sales. After typing in "post-apocalyptic," I might see "survival fiction" added to the end. (I will; I've searched it enough to know.) That is one keyword I'd accept and write down in Notepad. But I'd need more. That's a tough keyword to rank in, so I still need to niche down. I might try, "post-apocalyptic nuc" and see if "nuclear" shows up. If it does, great! That's a bona fide keyword. If not, we keep going.

I want "nuclear" in a longtail keyword. I already have "post-apocalyptic" with the first keyword, so it's locked down. You only need each keyword once. Amazon will ignore duplicates. My next try could be "survival fiction" or "prepper survival fiction." Again, I'd add "nuc" and see if it shows up if it didn't the last time. I would repeat that process until I had a good list of keywords. Amazon gives you seven keyword slots when uploading books, plus your title and subtitle hold keywords, arguably the best keywords. Each keyword slot allows 50 characters.

That's why you see a lot of non-fiction books start with "Make Money Online" or "Keto Diet," then the subtitle will be more descriptive but also contain keywords. The keywords in the title and subtitle are thought to contain more weight in Amazon's search results. Nobody can say for sure, but some tests have shown they could contain more weight. Still some say it's not true at all. I say, "It can't hurt to put your most important keywords in the title and subtitle." If it's true, you're set. If it's not, no worries. You've lost nothing.

In fiction, it's usually reversed. Staying with my theme here, a title would read, "Nuclear Dawn" and the subtitle would read, "A Post-Apocalyptic Survival Story." Again, that was off the top of my head.

Nuclear Dawn is a series by Kyla Stone. Her subtitle reads, *The Post-Apocalyptic Box Set: The Complete Apocalyptic Survival Thriller Series.* Notice how her subtitle is keyword rich but doesn't sound spammy. That's a talent you must learn. I count eight keywords. I'm impressed.

The study to end all studies... about Amazon keywords.

Dave Chesson, the Kindlepreneur, did a keyword study using self-published authors and their live books on Amazon. You can read the whole thing here, and I do recommend it: kevinbarry-maguire.com/7-Kindle-Keywords. He's giving away valuable information there. There has always been a debate on whether we should jam as many keywords into the 7 slots as possible or put one longtail keyword on each line.

Dave found out that you should use one longtail keyword on each line... for one to three of the slots. In the remaining slots, start cramming them in there! He also verified that you do not need to repeat a keyword. Amazon won't penalize you for repeating words, but you're wasting valuable real estate by doing so. If you have a phrase that wouldn't look right without a repeated word, use it. Dave uses "war mage" and "fantasy mage" as examples in the article. Since you will rank higher for the full terms than if they were spread out, use the full terms in those cases.

Case Study

Let's walk through the keyword research for real. I'll be using Amazon.com in a Chrome browser with the AMZ Suggestion Expander (Chrome Extension) available here: bit.ly/AMZ-Suggest. I'll search keywords for a post-apocalyptic book dealing with a nuclear attack. For added fun, I'm going to throw in "short reads" and see what hits I get. We'll get into short reads later in the KDP chapter.

My first search will start with the main keyword "post-apoca-lyptic" with "Kindle Store" selected in the dropdown. I like to see if anything new pops up in the keywords. Don't use quotes when looking for keywords. Amazon will only search the exact phrase, and your results will be minimal to non-existent. So, unless you want that exact phrase, don't use quotes.

Figure 2-1

As you can see in figure 2-1, the "survival fiction" showed up as normal. It's also at the top, making it the most searched for phrase. The column on the left is what Amazon will show you on a normal search. Everything to the right is the AMZ Suggestion

Expander. Normally there are more columns. What's missing from that list are some keywords I used for my previous books, "post apocalyptic fiction" being one of them.

"Nuclear" is not on the list, but I searched it anyway, using "post apocalyptic survival fiction nuclear" as the search string. It returned over 1000 results, which is low and right in the sweet spot for a beginner. The top result is the Nuclear Dawn boxed set, coincidentally. I'm not following the author around, I promise. It has a best-seller rank (BSR) of 3,555. I've been there before and know she's getting good sales and page reads. She has more in the top ten of this search too (four of them!) She's doing very well. The tenth book has a BSR of 34,098. This is a great category to write in, but I already knew that! When researching keywords for eBooks, you're looking for anything BSR of under 100,000. So that is going to be my main keyword and will be in the subtitle.

Now I have seven keyword boxes to fill. One of the keywords that didn't show up in the first search was dystopian. So, I typed it in and got over 10,000 results. That is not an easy keyword to rank in. The top result has a BSR of 27,899 and the tenth book is 12,753. I don't know what's going on there. It's like it's backward day on Amazon. The last three books on the page had BSR's of 2020, 974, and 511. That last one is a fantasy book by Nora Roberts. That makes as much sense as a reverse BSR ranking.

I noticed the top result was another series I've read, The Forager, by Peter R Stone. It's another great series. Just so you know, I've read some bad ones too. We won't be finding them on page one, however.

Back to keywords! I will use this keyword because I have four books using it already and an email list of previous buyers. I don't mind competing here. If you're a beginner, use it if you have room because you never know what might happen.

Searching "dystopian" by itself in the Amazon search box

yielded the same results as "post apocalyptic fiction." Only "dystopian" was in front of all the suggestions. The Suggestion Expander had a few more results, but they included the dreaded 'F' word, free! You can't use that word in your keywords. Other words you can't use: Amazon, Kindle, KDP Select, Kindle Unlimited, best-seller, and others, or brand names. It sucks because I spent several months as a best-seller in multiple categories and would love to be able to use that as a keyword. I was able to use several of those keywords for this book, however. I emailed KDP ahead of time and gave them the rundown of this book.

Another keyword I used previously was "prepper fiction." I don't suggest you give away your keywords when you find them. I do suggest you keep them close to your chest. Like I said, I have an email list. So I typed that in, and you can see the results in figure 2-2.

Figure 2-2 Keywords

One I don't remember seeing before is "teotwawki prepper fiction." It means, "the end of the world as we know it." It's prepper lingo for when the country/world sees an apocalyptic event. I've used it in other places and was surprised that I had not used it for any of my books. I just checked because I was curious.

If you're old enough, that song is in your head now. Thank me or curse me, whichever applies.

So, I will be adding it to my list. I have used "shtf prepper fiction" and will add it to my growing list. I guess you want me to tell you what "shtf" means. Ok, break my arm… shit hit the fan. That's bugout time. Oh boy, now you want to know what that means too? Bugout means to grab your bugout bag and get the hell out of Dodge. Also a prepper term. You'll all be preppers by the time we're done here!

You see a few of the banned keywords, so skip the "free" and "Kindle" suggestions. You'll also notice "survival" spelled wrong. It's a sad state in America when a misspelled word is in the suggestion list. Amazon isn't fond of misspelled words in your keyword list, so you probably shouldn't use them.

"Box set" is a great keyword if… IF… you have a box set. Here's the problem with that keyword. Amazon hates it. You can't use it unless you're actually selling a box set, like movies or music. It comes in a box. You can use "bundle" for eBooks when you bundle two or more books into one. I'll cover that later. They won't allow it for paperbacks, however. I'll cover that later too.

The last one I've used before was "apocalyptic." When I searched Amazon for it today, it returned the same results as our earlier searches. One difference is "romance" was number two on the list. That will be good for romance writers. My series have a male and female lead, and they're in a relationship, but it is *not* a romance or even a love story. So it would be bad for me to use "romance" as a keyword. It has no relevance and would hurt my rankings. Never use keywords that aren't relevant to your book, shirt, video, etc.

So far, we have the subtitle keyword and three extras. We need more, at least seven more. Seven? But that makes ten keywords!

If you aren't old enough, I bet you looked up that song and now it's in your head too. It was the eighties, I'm not proud.

You've seen the lists, so how are we going to get seven more keywords out of them? Easy. We're going to look at the search results and find more keywords in the titles, descriptions, and browse paths.

Figure 2-3

As you can see above, I searched "post apocalyptic fiction nuclear," and the first result is a bundle from our friend, Kyla. So now I'm going to click on her title and go to the product page. When doing this kind of research, don't click on advertisements. Other authors are paying for each click they get, and Amazon doesn't know you're only doing research. It's bad form.

I've already mentioned her subtitle was keyword rich, so now let's break them down and see if there is anything I can add to my list.

"Complete" is a keyword, people look for "complete sets." The book I'm going to write will be the first in a short-read series. So that keyword is certainly not relevant for me here. How about "Apocalyptic Survival?" You bet. "Thriller Series?" I'm not sure if that will fit yet, so I'm leaving it out. Put them all together for a longtail keyword, "The Complete Apocalyptic Survival Thriller Series."

We'll test them all out and see what happens. You'll notice I kept "series" in there. It is a series, even book one can be called a series if you're planning on more books. That's the next step, after we find enough keywords.

I read her description, and at the bottom is a good keyword from a review, "Awesome dystopian thriller with lots…" I'm writing "dystopian thriller" on my list. Who am I kidding? It's in Notepad, so I'm going to copy and paste it right in there. Who writes anymore? Not me. I get writers' cramp just signing my name these days.

Figure 2-4

I checked out her browse paths, the ranked lines under "Amazon Best Sellers Rank" and some a few interesting keywords I can use for this book. They don't apply to my Aftermath series, however. "Teen and Young Adult Dystopian eBooks" and "Teen and Young Adult Apocalyptic and Post-Apocalyptic eBooks." Those look very interesting to me and are being added to the list. My lead character will be a young adult. I'm thinking a ripe 22 years old.

Side note: This is also how you will find your book categories should you choose to go the book route.

Now it's time to move on to the next book: *Trackers: The Complete Four Book Series (A Post-Apocalyptic Survival Thriller.)* I think you can see the keywords in there now and understand why I'm moving on to the description without comment. The only thing I saw in the description was "EMP attack." EMP is electromagnetic pulse and will not work for me. A nuclear blast will set off an EMP, but not on a large scale, which is what people interested in the genre are looking for. So, it's only about 10% relevant for me, not enough.

The browse paths aren't interesting, but I'll use "Men's Adventure Fiction" and see what happens. The other two are the same thing except for women – one for eBooks and one for Books. (Paperback.) Let's try another one.

Next... well, after another Kyla book... is *Forager – The Complete Six Book Series (A Post Apocalyptic/Dystopian Series*. Again, we have that title covered. I skipped a book because it was another Kyla Stone book, and I didn't think we'd get much more out of it. Unfortunately, this book is set in the future and falls under science fiction. I didn't find anything useful and need to move on. It's okay though; this is normal operating procedure.

The next volunteer is *Get Out Alive: A Post-Apocalyptic Survival Thriller (Atomic Threat Book 2.)* There is nothing in the title and description for me, and I struck out on the browse paths. Nothing new there. I'm looking for just a few more keywords, and one of these books will have what I need. I'm going to skip titles that come up empty from here out.

After digging through several pages, because Kyla Stone takes half of the first page, I found three more keywords. Man, she is kicking all kinds of butt! I thought her books were good, and I'm not the only one. Whew. So, I added "nuclear warheads," "nuclear attack," and "the end of the world as we know it." That's teotwawki spelled out and another round of that song stuck in our heads.

So now it's time to verify our keywords by searching them on Amazon. When doing this, make sure "Kindle Store" is selected in the dropdown box of the search bar. For paperbacks, you'll want "Books" selected. The first one we're going to search is, "teotwawki prepper fiction." Doh! There it is again!

I've completed the search and looked at three numbers:

Search results, BSR of the #1 and #10 books. The search results tell you how much competition there is in the keyword. A result of 1000 or less is great, especially for beginners. A result of 10,000 or more is crazy competition. I found keywords representing both the high and low and some in between. I'll grab another screenshot to show you where to look. Always remember not to count ads in any of your research (and don't click on them!) They aren't part of a natural result.

Figure 2-5

As you can see in figure 2-5, the results show up on the top left, and the BSR shows up under the cover photo. You'll see a BSR of 1375 on several of the results. If you can't figure out the author, you haven't been paying attention. She's everywhere!

teotwawki prepper fiction 496|4723|55,594
   shtf prepper fiction 1000|48,333|151,668
   Apocalyptic Survival 8000|1375|23,459
   The Apocalyptic Survival Series 5000|5342|7628
   Teen and Young Adult Dystopian eBooks 10,000|1375|Unk

Teen and Young Adult Apocalyptic and Post-Apocalyptic eBooks 3000|1375|18,446

Men's Adventure Fiction 40,000|367|247

Nuclear Warheads 60|837,063|4,248,273

Nuclear attack 493|1982|3087

the end of the world as we know it 139|88,232|355,729

Right off the bat, we see teotwawki prepper fiction only has 496 search results. Amazing! The number one book in the keyword has a BSR of 4,723, and the number ten book's BSR is only 55,594. This is a winner!

Keywords I won't be using? "Men's Adventure Fiction," 40,000 results and BSR's under 500? No thanks! That's a fist-fight, as my friend and mentor, Dale L Roberts would say. More on him later. "Nuclear warheads" looks cool with that search result of 60, but that's where the awesome ends. The number one book there is a whopping 837,063 and ten is 4,248,273. Nobody is buying those books. It will do no good to rank for a keyword nobody is buying.

Now, we'll go through the rest and see what we can do. I can knock one more out but may have room for all of them. When we look at "shtf prepper fiction" we see 1000 search results and BSR's of 48,333 and 151,668. The first two are good, but that last one is a bit worrying. Remember, we want our results to stay under 100,000. So that one is off to the side for now.

"Apocalyptic survival" has 8,000 results and BSR's of 1,375 and 23,459. The search results aren't ideal for a beginner or a first book in a series, but the other two numbers look great. I'm going to harp on it again here – an email list is a game changer. While mine is a first book in a series, I collect email addresses from readers in all my books. No matter what you're selling, having an email list makes it a lot easier. More on that later, however; including where to get started for free.

Now we get to "Teen and Young Adult Dystopian eBooks." This one is interesting. The search resulted in 10,000 books and a top BSR of 1,375. But the BSR for the tenth (and a lot more) books is nonexistent. No sales. It doesn't make sense to me how a book with zero sales is number ten and a book under 5,000 is number 12. It still looks like a fist fight though. It's a maybe, if there is room.

"Teen and Young Adult Apocalyptic and Post-Apocalyptic eBooks" looks more promising. It only has 3,000 results and BSR's of 1,375 and 18,446. This is a winner. Nuclear attack is another winner; I'll take it. "The end of the world as we know it" is another one that looks cool with only 139 results. But the number one book has a pretty high BSR, and the number ten is very high. I don't think people are searching for this term, and they aren't buying it. I pray this is the last time that song is getting stuck in our heads, but I can't make promises.

That leaves me with my title and subtitle and five boxes to fill with keywords. I have two boxes remaining, and I will stuff them with generic stuff, "for teens" "for boys" (and girls) and things of that nature. You will have to think of your audience, who will want to buy your book, and put it in there. Remember, no quotation marks! If you have extra keywords from your searching, you can put those in the remaining boxes too. Don't be shy.

This chapter was more detailed than I expected. Whew, I need a break!

Dave Chesson has an article on how to choose keywords that I'm sure you'll get value from: https://kevinbarrymaguire.com/Choose-Keywords.

Chapter 2 Exercises

You get to search Dale's favorite example search term: Werebear shapeshifter romance. Don't laugh, it's a real genre with devoted fans. If you have something else in mind, be my guest. Find your subtitle, remember in fiction the keywords are in the subtitle. Then fill three to five slots with longtail keywords, and the rest with smaller or generic keywords. Make a good list, then verify them. Decide which are keepers and which are not. Take action.

CHAPTER 3 SOFTWARE

Software makes our jobs much easier, and there is a lot of software to be used in the chapters ahead. I want to detail them here, so I won't have to break stride mid-chapter later. I'll start off with the free software, because I think a lot of you won't have money to spare on a lot of software.

The paid software will follow, and they can add up. So stick with free while you're getting started, and switch to paid when you're making money. There are a few you may want to purchase right from the start, but that's a decision for you to make.

Free

AMZ Suggestion Expander is one I've already mentioned, so it's a good one to start off with. It also starts with "A," making it appear that I'm organized enough to alphabetize the list. I'll smash that illusion after a few software suggestions. This is the Chrome extension that adds to the suggestions in an Amazon search. It will give you words before and after the keyword you're searching for. This is probably the most useful extension you can get for selling on Amazon. It is a must.

Once you install it, that's all you ever have to do. Whenever you type a keyword into the Amazon search bar, the extension will automatically give the extra suggestions. Hands-free, worry free.

DS Amazon Quickview is another Chrome extension and saves you a lot of time in research. You can get it here: bit.ly/Amazon-Quickview. If you remember my photos from the previous chapter, the BSR showed up on the search page. That's not normal. That's DS Amazon Quickview helping us out. Without the extension, a person must click on the book/shirt/whatever and scroll down to the product details to see the BSR. With the extension, you'll see it immediately, no clicking! This is another must have for your research.

Eye Dropper is great when you see a color on the Internet that you'd like to use in one of your designs. Download it here: bit.ly/Dropper-Tool. Don't freak out; the designs aren't difficult. You don't need to be a designer to do any of this. It helps, for sure, but isn't necessary.

Using this tool is confusing at first. It appears as an eyedropper over a square box. The color of the box changes as you use it. It's the color of the last time you used it. First, click on the eyedropper tool, then choose "Pick color from web page." It's a box on the upper left.

Figure 3-1

Your mouse pointer will have a square box under it, and the tip of the pointer is what is choosing the color. Once you're happy with the color showing in the box, left click. It looks like nothing happened, but it did! Click on the extension again (you'll notice the color you chose is now the box color on the extension bar.)

Now you'll see those boxes on the right with all the numbers, are the color you chose. Now copy and paste the code you need into the design software you're using. It will also be saved for a while in the palette.

I've never even looked at what "Plus" does so I'm guessing I don't need it. The free version does everything I need. Most likely, it will for you too.

Pretty Merch is a very nice Chrome extension used for Merch by Amazon, kevinbarrymaguire.com/Pretty-Merch. Just about everyone who does Merch by Amazon uses Pretty Merch. It has both a free and Pro version. The pro version is a paid version, and I'll talk about those features later in the chapter. The free version is a must for everyone doing Merch.

Pretty Merch gives you a new tab on the Merch site and gives you an overview of your current sales. It shows you how many sales you've received "today" in a box on the left. That box also shows you "Sold," "Cancelled," "Returned," and "Royalties." Everything you need at a glance for the day. Don't worry, in the almost two years I've been at this, I've only had six returns and 11 cancellations. It's nothing to worry yourself over. You'll spend more time worrying about what to binge watch next on Netflix.

To the right of that box is a seven-day graph, showing your daily sales for the past seven days, including the current day. It shows you sales, the bars, and royalties, the red line. Today, I'm currently showing one sale, but the royalty line is far above the bar. It's because it's a $19.99 shirt, one of the few I have. It's also the ugliest shirt I have. It sells. A lot. Don't worry about your design skills. Worry about the manatees and marshmallow clouds.

Under those two items, there are three tabs on the left that show you which shirts sold today, top units sold, and which shirts are giving you the top royalties. To the right of that is your sales information, the current counts. It shows yesterday, the last seven days, this month, previous month, and all time.

Up at the top of the page, it will show you what Tier you're in. I'm Tier 500, meaning I'm allowed 500 designs live on Amazon. When my all-time sales reach 500, I'll be tiered up to 1000. They also have a little cartoon monster representing each tier. I'm showing an orange puffball monster.

Next to that is your upload status. Under review, processing, and rejected, it will show you how many designs are in each stage. I'll talk about rejections in the Merch chapter. Very short version, be cool, and you'll be alright… alright, alright.

Bringing up the rear are circles with the US, UK, and German flags with numbers representing sales in each area. Mine will always show US only. I'm not uploading to the other two, explained later.

The bonus! As long as you're logged in, Pretty Merch will give an audible "cha-ching!" every time you make a sale. It's an awesome sound that I will never get tired of. You'll also get a popup box telling you which shirt or PopSocket sold, but that's a Windows notification.

That is all great information at your fingertips for free. The Pro version does much more.

Canva, canva.com, is an image processing app, like Photoshop without nearly all the bells and whistles, but it's free. They also have a paid version, of course. It's great if you don't have something else or have zero ability to use a stronger program, like Photoshop, Affinity Photo, or Gimp… to name a few. Before I got Photoshop, this is what I used. Gimp was too difficult for me, and I never thought to use YouTube to learn how to use it. That's how I learned Photoshop, by the way. Now I use Affinity Photo and Affinity Designer for photos and other images.

You start Canva by choosing an image size – poster, card, business card, Instagram, etc. Then it will take you to the edit page. From there, you choose a template or click the other tabs to design on your own. One good thing about Canva, the templates are good, very good. They have free and paid templates, and they're all good. The paid ones are $1, and I think I read they're free if you pay for Canva. It's all self-explanatory for the most part. It's a very easy process to learn.

That brings me to Gimp, gimp.org, as I stated a few minutes ago, I tried Gimp and got lost. It was four or five years ago. I think I'd find it easy today because of my experience with photoshop. I deleted the program ages ago so I can't say for sure. I know Dale L Roberts used it exclusively until a few months ago. I've seen a lot of the stuff he's done with it, and it's top quality. I can't tell you if it's missing anything Photoshop or Affinity can do, however. It's available on Windows, GNU/Linux, and OS X.

I would recommend this over Canva any day of the week. You can watch YouTube videos to learn how to use it, and when I visited their website, I saw they have tutorials. I don't know if they had them when I first downloaded it. In my naivete, I probably didn't think to look.

Instead of leaving it at, "duh, gee George. I don't know," I read some articles comparing the two. One, at expertphotography.com, I saw the deal breaker. If you're going to do print on demand (POD) then you will need Photoshop or Affinity Photo. Gimp does not use CYMK colors, only RGB. RGB is for the web; CYMK is for printing. Merch is POD, as is Ignite. But Amazon still demands RGB from our designs. But most printers will want CYMK. Barnes and Noble will only accept CYMK for your book covers. GIMP and Photoshop cannot do that. Affinity and Adobe Illustrator will.

Google Docs, google.com/docs/about, is one I used and

didn't like very much. I think that's just a personal preference. Other people I know like it just fine. This goes for their entire suite. Slides, sheets, and more. I spent most of my life in the state of Washington, Steilacoom and Lakewood to be specific. I have friends that work at Microsoft, and I like to support the local economy. Windows is making that difficult, however. Those forced updates have me wanting to throw my computer out the window! It has me thinking Mac more and more, and I'm *not* a Mac guy. I am an iPhone guy though. But I digress.

I'm sure Google Docs is just fine to write in, and they probably have all the bells and whistles Word has. The thing is, I know Word very well. I know Excel very well, and I know PowerPoint very well. Learning it all again for Google just isn't in the cards for me. One thing Google doesn't have, however, are the Kindle plugins for Word. Those are free plugins from Amazon that will format your books for you.

That brings me to Word, products.office.com/en-us/home. I like it. I bet that comes as a surprise to you. I've been using the Office suite since there was an Office suite. Instead of purchasing Office 2016, I pay the $6.99 monthly fee for Office 365 Personal. It's always updated with the newest bells and whistles and just like Google, I can save docs to the cloud via One Drive. That's the only way to autosave now, which is a minus in my book. It should autosave no matter how I choose to save the document.

I'll mention PowerPoint here too, because if you plan on doing some of the things I talk about in the KDP chapter, you might want PowerPoint. I have used Slides recently, and it will probably work just as well as PowerPoint, but I can't be sure. I never used Slides for interiors. Once again, I can do anything in PowerPoint and might get hung up in Slides. Besides, if you get Word, you get PowerPoint in the package, so the decision is easy in that case.

Kindle Create, Kindle Kids Book Creator, and Kindle Comic Creator are all individual software available for free from

Amazon. Kindle Create also has the plugin for Word, a valuable plugin for sure. These programs format your books to epub (Amazon's eBook format) and format for paperback. If you're writing children's books, use the Kids Book Creator. If you've made some comics, use the Comic Creator. For everything else, use Kindle Create.

The Kindle Create plugin for Word is awesome. You set up the document in the Kindle tab before typing anything. When your book is finished, you click a button, and the plugin turns your .docx into an .epub and makes the file ready for uploading as a paperback. It inserts page numbers and sets the margins. Page numbering manually can be a pain in the rear; it has made me scream more than once. I'd rather roll naked on a bed of nails and take a bath in lemon juice than worry about page numbers again.

Lunapic, www4.lunapic.com/editor/, (yes, you need the "4") is a web-based photo editing software that I use for background removal. But it does a lot more. You can convert a file format, say from .png to .jpg. You can crop, skew, scale, adjust colors. You can even draw, add watermarks and borders, and a whole lot more. I've never really explored it all though. I only use it for erasing backgrounds because in Affinity Photo and Designer, it's not an easy thing to do. Well, it is. It's just… involved. Layer masks are involved. In Lunapic, it's very easy.

Paid

Now I'll discuss some software that will cost you a little coin. Some are paid monthly – with yearly options, and some are one-time fees. Everything I discuss here I bought and use or used until I bought a replacement. That last part applies to Photoshop. I bought a replacement. These programs will make your life a lot easier, but remember, there are free alternatives if you don't have the money.

I'll start off with Pretty Merch Pro because I've already given you some good details on the free version of Pretty Merch, kevin-barrymaguire.com/Pretty-Merch. I took a bunch of screenshots back in December 2019 when I first started making the outline for this book. It's now February 2020, and my total sales are 315. Remember, I need 500 to tier up. One of the following photos will show much fewer sales.

Figure 3-2

You'll notice on the top right, it says Pretty Merch Pro. I ain't jacking my jaws about having all the paid software I'm discussing. I also notice something I didn't mention when discussing the free version. The blur feature. Both versions have it, and as you can see, it blurs out your designs and title so you can post photos without anyone being able to steal your work. Obviously, a great feature.

You can also see I am Tier 500, and I have a rejection. I made an awesome design that said, "Jeffrey Epstein Didn't Kill Himself." Only a few people were selling the shirts when I saw it on Amazon. Mine was better than theirs because I made mine in Affinity Designer and put some effects on the text. Amazon said I couldn't use names with copyright. I told them there were no trademarks on his name (I looked beforehand, of course) and nobody can copyright a name. They didn't care. I asked why other people could use his name. I was told they couldn't discuss other people. Hmm…

Figure 3-3

The Analytics tab on Pretty Merch Pro is awesome. This is the previous year, but you can also look at today, yesterday, last 7 days, last 14 days, this month, previous month, last 90 days, year to date, all time, and custom.

Below the graph is a wealth of information. It gives you sales, returns, royalties, and royalties per sale. You get averages, record days and months, and a whole lot more. Images to the rescue!

Figure 3-4

Figure 3-4 shows what is immediately under the graph. This isn't a full year, obviously. I've done five sales in a day three or four times. I thought I would do more in December, but maybe next time. For sure next time, I'll be Tier 1000 by then.

Figure 3-5

Figure 3-5 shows the next part of the results. Unique Products Sold (circled) is how many individual designs sold in the period. You can have 48 sales, but 26 unique products. When a design sells once, it's unique. It can sell ten more times in the period, but it's only unique once.

The 80/20 rule means 20% of your products will produce 80% of your sales. It doesn't seem to work for me. You can also see I don't sell very many PopSockets. I need to increase my designs there. I sell mostly men's shirts, and the top color is black. It's always black. For everyone. When I make my designs, I always make sure they look good on black.

Below, this is a list of all the designs that sold during the period in question. I can't show you that list because it would be a bunch of blurred out images and text.

The next tab in Pretty Merch Pro is Products. This is pretty cool! You can search your inventory by title or ASIN (Amazon's assigned number to products on their site.) You can choose your marketplace, United States, United Kingdom, or Germany. If you choose "More Filters" you get a whole host of other options. The ones I like best are "Has Sold" and "Pending Removal." It helps me decide what designs I'm going to delete to make room for new ones. That will be explained in the Merch chapter.

In the product list blurred out in the photo, you'll see dollar bills, if they're green, the design has sold. When greyed out, no dice. The flag tells you which marketplace it's in, and you can edit and delete from this page instead of the Merch product tab. Like I said, knowing if a product has sold or is about to drop off is great information. You get none of that on Amazon's Merch page. When a design gets close, Merch will show it on the product list, but you can't search for it like you can in Pretty Merch Pro. As you can see, I love this extension!

Publisher Rocket, kevinbarrymaguire.com/Publisher-Rocket, is some pretty awesome software made by Dave Chesson. Remember that long keyword chapter? Of course, you do. It was the previous chapter, and you're a smart cookie. Imagine if you could do all that research in a matter of minutes? You can with Publisher Rocket. Hopefully, you did your homework in the

Keyword chapter, because you need to know how to do it manually. If you haven't done it yet, why not? Take action.

Figure 3-6

Image 3-6, above, shows the main screen you see after opening the software. You can do keyword research, competition analyzer, category search, and game changing AMS Keyword Search. If you thought keyword research was an involved process, imagine trying to find up to 1000 keywords for an ad campaign? Publisher Rocket takes care of that in seconds. Then you download the csv file and upload it to your ad campaign during setup. Easier than scraping the cream of an Oreo cookie with your teeth.

I'll get more into the other two options later in the book. This software isn't required to run a publishing business, but it sure makes life easier and saves a *ton* of time. Notice I didn't say "author business" or "writing career." Remember, you don't have to write books to publish books. It's easier than you think, and I will be showing you how, in detail. **Preview**: Did you know you can publish a book without words? Get ready, it's awesome, and it's part of the next chapter. Hold on to your hats!

The Affinity Suite, affinity.serif.com/en-gb/designer, includes Designer, Photo, and Publisher. These are alternative software to Adobe Illustrator, Photoshop, and InDesign... in that order. Each of these programs are sold separately for $49.99 each. I was paying Adobe $9.99 a month alone for Photoshop. I didn't have the other two and didn't know I needed them. Man, was I wrong. A vector program (Designer and Illustrator) make much higher quality designs because you can resize a vector to any size without reducing quality. You can't do that with a .png or .jpg file. Which means, Photoshop is not ideal for anything but photographs.

I bought all three of the Affinity products when they were on sale. You can catch them for $40 each if you're patient. Black Friday was even cheaper. As I'll explain later, my business exploded when I started using Designer.

I'll pay a monthly fee if I must, but when I read up on how good the Affinity products were, I ditched the monthly payment and got *much more*. With Designer, I can make higher quality t-shirt designs (even if it's just text) than I could with Photoshop. I can make better designs to sell on stock sites. Photoshop is great for photos, probably the best. *But that's it*. It cannot do what Designer or Illustrator does.

Affinity Publisher is a document program. If you know what InDesign does, you know what Publisher does. You can use it to format books, pamphlets, magazines, posters, and the like. I used to make my journal interiors with PowerPoint, and they're good. Now I use Publisher, and they're great. I can also do it much faster, which is hard to believe since I'm an expert in PowerPoint. I'm a novice in Publisher. It's that good.

As for Affinity Photo, I can't say much yet. I haven't used it except to play around once. You can remove objects from a photo just by drawing over them. It's amazing. No layer masks! On the downside, you cannot remove a background without a layer mask like you can in Photoshop. That's coming down the road, I think.

Just when you thought you heard it all, it gets better. If you have two or all three of the programs, *you can use them inside the one you currently have open*. This is huge. While working in Publisher, if

I need to edit a photo in Photo, I just switch to the Photo persona (a cool way of saying "tab" in Affinity lingo) and bam, I have everything I need. It's a little different if you're working in Photo or Designer, you have to go to File > Edit in Photo (or Designer.) The reason being is those two programs have other personas included.

These programs cannot do everything their Adobe counterparts can, but they won't ding your bank account every month either – and all their updates/upgrades are free. Affinity is continually updating their products to make them better, so I see a day when they will have just as much as Adobe's products. The only thing I miss about Photoshop is the background eraser tool. It can be done in Photo, but Lunapic is faster.

Vellum is a very nice program that formats beautiful book interiors, kevinbarrymaguire.com/Vellum. It has one downside: it's Mac only. That can be fixed, however. I have a PC but use MacInCloud to access Vellum, macincloud.com. Easy as pie. Although, I tried to bake a pie once. It's not that easy. But MacInCloud is. I can format my book interiors by hand if I must. I'll avoid it at all costs, however. I can format in Kindle Create, and it will take less time than manual and look nice. Or I can speed up the process considerably and have a beautiful interior that I know will be accepted by everyone – including Ingram Spark. Their pdf standards are high.

Vellum has two price points, regular for eBooks and $50 more for both eBooks and Paperbacks. It's a no-brainer to pay the extra for both, that's what I did. Of course, I write and publish both formats. This is only for those of you who will follow the publishing path – fiction and nonfiction. There are other publishing aspects you will learn that don't involve writing or even words. I'm going to hold you in suspense on that until the next chapter. No peeking.

Figure 3-7

Figure 3-8

Figure 3-7 shows the MacIncloud desktop, which you can see is a Mac desktop. It's very empty on mine because I only use it for Vellum. I pay by the minute while logged into MacInCloud, so I will only use it for something that makes me money.

Figure 3-8 is what Vellum looks like with a document loaded. This is the lasted book I finished. Vellum creates the table of contents for you and takes care of the page numbers. It will make sure all chapters start on the correct side for paperback. That's another hassle I didn't mention before.

You can do a lot with the chapter titles, and there is a collection of decorations you can use under the chapter title. They also show up in chapter breaks if you use an ellipse as a separator. There is a lot more Vellum can do. It's an amazing piece of software that I can't live without now.

I think everyone knows what Microsoft Office is; at least, those of us who haven't just arrived from Venus. I bet you thought I was going to say, "Mars." Cliché ain't my jam. There are only two Office programs I use in my business, and one took a backseat to Affinity Publisher. But Word is what I write most of my books in. I also use Scrivener, but only for my fiction writing. I'll talk about that next. You already know about the Kindle Create addon, and that's a huge bonus for Word over Google or Open Office.

PowerPoint is the other one, and that is used to make the journal interiors. Affinity Publisher or Adobe's InDesign is a better option. If you don't want either of those programs, however; PowerPoint will get the job done. Its downfall is speed. It's a much slower process in PowerPoint, and you can get more done in less time with the other two programs. This should come as no surprise, but the more you have up for sale, the more money you're going to make.

Scrivener is a monster of a program, kevinbarrymaguire.com/Scrivener. Most people who have it use it for all their writing. I only use it for my fiction because it helps me stay organized. I can look at character cards and remember the characters at a glance. My books have a large cast, keeping everyone straight after a few months of not writing about them can be difficult. Not anymore.

I can keep my maps in there too, and I use a lot of maps while writing. The other option is to have Google Maps open in a browser window. But the idea of Scrivener is not to leave the software – improving your words per minute.

There is a writing mode that gives you the full screen – no distractions – and keeps the curser about mid-screen, so your eyes aren't going from top to bottom. It's nice; I do love that. The full screen is another tool to keep distractions away. You'd be amazed at what you'll want to look at instead of writing. It all leads to a more words per hour count. I really should be using it for all my writing, but I like Word; what can I say? This book is written in Word.

Scrivener can also format your books for you, but I've never tried it. I'd already had Vellum when I purchased Scrivener. I do know others who have both and use Vellum to format their books. I don't think Scrivener has all of Vellum's bells and whistles. Crap, cliché!

Scrivener does much more; check it out if you think it will work for you. Again, this is only for actual books... with words.

That wraps up the software I use, or most of it. There are a few others I'll get to later. They're good but don't really need to be talked about separately.

Chapter 3 Exercises

It wasn't easy deciding on what homework to give you here. It wasn't that kind of chapter. But I promised to get you to take action in every chapter, so here it is. Compare the free versions of software to their paid counterparts and try to decide which ones will suit you best.

When just starting out, the free versions will work for most everyone. Try to think ahead when you're no longer a novice and see what you can figure out.

CHAPTER 4 KINDLE DIRECT PUBLISHING

*W*hat is Kindle direct publishing (KDP) and how can you make money with it? That's a good question, and I'm glad you asked! KDP is how you publish books on Amazon. Slow down! Don't run away yet; you'll be fine. Not all books are the same, and not all books have words in them. The kinds of books I'm talking about start with no content, just lines. Those are the notebooks and are the easiest to create. In fact, at the end of the book, I'll give you a chance to get some free templates, so you won't even have to worry about making the interiors. I've got you covered.

The next step up are the low content journals. These are designed around topics like wedding planners, all other types of planners, baby showers, religious, reunions, or just about anything else. These usually have some kind of prompts in them to spur the writing process, but they don't have to. They can be charts to write things like a to-do list, appointments, etc.

Then of course, you can write your own book with lots of words or even just a few words. Have you heard of Kindle short reads? They're awesome. You can write short books, and Amazon will put them in the short read categories for you. They're broken down by minutes and go up to over two hours. You can write ten- or fifteen-minute books and sell them on Amazon. This is how I started.

I've also written longer books. I have some other non-fiction books and the fourth book in my *Aftermath* series is a full novel. The first three are short reads. All the reviews kept saying, "Too short." So, I had to keep making them longer and longer.

Just when you thought the news couldn't get any better, it does! If you can't write or don't want to write, you can hire a ghost writer to do it for you. They do all the work; you take all the credit and royalties. The only downside there is you're going to start in the red. So, you'll have to do your research first and choose a very good keyword to go after. I know lots of people using this business model and are crushing it. I'm more of a hands-on guy, but there is no shame in hiring a writer. It still turns a profit; it just takes a little longer.

That is the hierarchy and the order I'll be discussing in this chapter. But first, I need to talk about the rules. Amazon is strict on their rules and will ban accounts for breaking them. Other people will steer you wrong here. I see it all the time on YouTube and in some courses. I think most everyone who teaches bad practices in their courses have lost their KDP account now. But they still have their courses out there for sale.

White Hat vs Black Hat

Why do we say white hat and black hat? It probably comes from old Hollywood Westerns, where the good guy always wore a white hat and Bad Bart and his ilk always had a black hat. So, white hat tactics are good, and black hat tactics are seen as bad, or cheating. I only use and teach white hat. I'm not going to lose my KDP account, and I won't be responsible for others losing theirs. Those guys teaching black hat don't care about other people. They're making their money and moving on.

Cheating the system may work for a little bit, but Amazon will catch on eventually, and they will terminate your account. Worse, when your account is terminated, they keep all the money they owe you. It's got to be a shock to the system. So, pay close attention here, and you'll be rocking those paychecks, worry-free.

Review swaps. Let's start with the biggest of them all. Amazon hates this practice. There are some who say, "Nobody lost their account due to review swaps," and they're wrong. Don't listen to them. There are still people telling you to do review swaps, in their courses and on YouTube. Don't listen to them.

A "review swap" isn't really a swap anymore. It's where you pay someone to write five-star reviews for your book. There are people out there with multiple Amazon accounts that will do it for you. Amazon has started suing people for doing it. They're also suing people who teach it in their courses. It's a big no-no.

It started out with authors reviewing each other's books. Hence, "swap." Amazon doesn't like that either, even if you read the book and leave an honest review for each other.

The white hat way of getting swaps is to ask your readers to leave an "honest review." **Do not ask for a "positive" review**, or a five-star review. Amazon will not be happy. You can only ask for an honest review.

If you have money to spare, because it's not cheap, you can go to https://www.netgalley.com and submit your book there. You will have no control over the types of reviews you get. They will be honest reviews, for better or worse. So, if you write some werebear shapeshifter romance, but you've never even read a single story in the genre, you can bet you're going to get lit up in the reviews. If you did your due diligence, you'll be ok.

Removing books from your dashboard and re-uploading

them. Amazon gives new books a chance to be seen over established books by giving a 30-day ratings boost to the books. It's a good thing Amazon is doing to help us with our new books. This goes for all books, notebooks included.

What some people do is remove a book that didn't sell well during the first 30 days and upload it again. They game the system hoping it will do better next time. But what they're doing is hurting other authors with new books and authors whose established books lose their ranking for those 30 days. Thirty days is fair; don't be a douche canoe.

Next is plagiarism. Don't do it. You lose your account and your credibility at the same time. Amazon checks for plagiarism with every upload, so don't think you're going to copy and paste your way to new books. Whether you write your own or pay someone to write for you, always do a plagiarism check. There are a few free ones online, but you get what you pay for. Grammarly and ProWritingAid both have plagiarism checks built in. It is an extra charge, but they're top notch. Both of those are professional editing software.

There have been a few major plagiarism scandals in the self-publishing world. The most recent was a woman brazen enough to steal Nora Roberts' content, then she blamed her ghostwriters for the theft! The writers fought back.

The newest black hat tactic going on, especially in the low and no content world, is copying titles, descriptions, and covers: Word for word and photo for photo. This is obviously against Amazon's terms of service.

There is a woman I know in a Facebook group who is going through this right now. She's got high ranking journals that people are copying and selling at a lower cost. They steal her interior, her cover, title, and description. She's complained to Amazon and is now in an appeal.

They have been slow to rectify the situation, however. But rest assured, when they do take action, accounts will be lost. It happens every time. People will get away with something for a while, then the hammer drops on their lives.

One day they're in the money, thinking of how they're going to spend their ill-gotten gains. Then poof! It's all gone. Gone because Amazon won't pay the royalties still waiting to be paid out. It's a few months' worth. Amazon pays authors two months after the sale, at the end of the month. So, you're looking at about a three month wait to get paid. If you break the rules, you won't get any of it. White hat is the way to go. FYI, people do this with shirts on Merch by Amazon too. Amazon is much quicker to delete accounts on Merch.

The last one I'll talk about is book stuffing. The idea here is to add "bonus" material to the end of the book and put the book in Kindle Select. That's where people can read the books for free if they sign up for Kindle Unlimited (KU.) I have it, and it's great.

When your book (words only, no journals and such) is in Kindle Select, you get paid by the page read. So, by adding the bonus material, they increase their page count and payday. This doesn't sound bad at first, and some people did it right. But there were others who would add tons of other books, sometimes not even their own. Worse, they would put links to the back of the book and have you go there first, ensuring every page got counted as "read."

Amazon has fixed the linking to the end and the bonus situation. You aren't allowed to have more than 10% of the book as bonus content.

I encourage you to read Amazon's terms of service so you don't get a nasty surprise one day. You can find the ToS here: https://bit.ly/AmzTos. And now, we get to the meat of the book, how you're going to make that money. Everything before this point is important; don't sleep on it. (That's another "Dale" term.) If anyone is trying to teach you how to do any of the bad stuff I mentioned, RUN! Run away fast, and don't look back.

I know this stuff is still being taught and even still taught by people who have lost their accounts already. Naming names is a tough situation. I want to; man, do I want to… but the legalities are in my way. I'll say one is a Canadian who doesn't live in Canada or the US. He *may* still have his account, but I doubt it. He also might have moved back to Canada. I stopped watching his channel months ago. I also ignore his Facebook group, though I'm still a member, I think.

Another one is… ones. Twins. That's all I can say. I liked them when they first came on the scene. One of them can't seem to keep any accounts. He lost his KDP account, his Merch account, and is ACX account. They both lost ACX. ACX doesn't even want to hear their names!

There are more, but I'll say this: I can't list all the good people in the industry; there are too many to list here. So, I can't say, "If I don't talk about them, they're suspect." But I can tell you that the people I *do* talk about, I have verified. I've purchased their courses and know what they teach. I've spent hours upon hours watching their YouTube videos.

The people I mention in this book are top notch. They're good people who won't steer you wrong.

No Content Books

Use the amazon search bar to do research and see what customers are searching for then create books around that data.

Too many people think of ideas in their head and just create them without validating the niche.

Using this method of looking to see what people are searching for, then creating books around that data gives you a much better chance of actually selling books because we are solving someone's problem.

People might be searching for a "charge nurse gift" so if we create a really pretty design for charge nurses on a journal and target the keywords "charge nurse gifts" then we have a much better chance of selling said book because that's what people are actually searching for.

Paddy from StackinProfit
kevinbarrymaguire.com/stackin-profit

Remember when I said you can create books with no words? Of course, you do. It was only a chapter ago. The most common "no-content" book is the lined notebook. Of those, college-rule is the most common. There is also wide-ruled and handwriting notebooks for kids. Those are the ones with two solid lines with a dotted line in the middle. If you were paying attention in the Keywords chapter, and I know you were because you're a superstar, you know I just mentioned a keyword – handwriting notebooks for kids.

Mine are 99% college-ruled, 6x9, and have 110 pages. Children's notebooks need to be 8x10 or 8.5x11. They need more room than us. I do have a few children's handwriting notebooks out there. You'll see some notebooks at 100 pages and some at 120, so why do I choose 100? It's not because it's in the middle. I'm not splitting the difference on purpose.

One-hundred pages isn't enough when lots of other people are selling 110 and 120 pages – and sometimes more! People see the page counts, and they're paying attention. Why would they pay $6.99 for 100 pages when they can pay the same price for 110 or more? A lot of times, they won't – unless they really like the cover. The cover is important. It's the only reason they're paying $6.99 on Amazon instead of $1 at the dollar store. But they usually have choices in covers.

Here's the deal. For black and white printing, Amazon gives

you the first 108 pages at a base cost. Everything from 24 pages (their minimum) to 108 pages costs $2.15 to print. After that, they charge $0.012 cents per page. So, to keep my profit margin at its highest point, while keeping a nice round number, I do 110 pages.

FYI, color is ridiculously high. That's why you don't see many color photos in books printed by Amazon. They don't charge per color page; they charge the whole book. The printing cost for 24-40 pages is $3.65. For color books with 42 to 500 pages, it's another seven cents per page. Now you know why children's books cost more. They're all printed in color.

At $6.99, your profit is $2.02 on a black and white notebook with 110 pages. I see you jumping up and down screaming, "Woohoo! Two dollars! I want my two dollars!" I know, it doesn't seem like a lot, but it does add up. The more quality notebooks and journals you put up, the more you're going to make. I know, I'm not preaching rocket science here. Just know that $2 can turn into $1000 per month with a little bit of research and effort. I've seen people hit that mark in a matter of months. There is a woman I'll talk about later who made $18,000 in one month – December. Pay attention to what she says; she's one of the experts giving tips in this book. Since I haven't added the tips yet, you may have met her already – Kelli Roberts, aka Kelli Publish - https://www.youtube.com/kellipublish.

I know another who is making $5000 a month after less than a year. I'll introduce him too. I'm only giving numbers from people who have made the numbers public themselves first. I'll say I've been doing more than $1000 a month since my second- or third-month publishing. I got a jumpstart by having the first book I ever wrote make it to #1 in several categories on Amazon. More on that later.

No and low-content publishing is a numbers game. I heard it said you need to have 1000 books uploaded to start making a decent income with no and low content books. That sounds like a lot, and it is... but it isn't. You're reusing the same interiors, and you aren't writing anything. The only thing you're doing each time is creating the covers, which I'll go over in this chapter. Even those can be duplicated somewhat. Of course, you're going to need to find the keywords too.

Some people can upload ten a day with no issues. Some people upload 100 a day. That boggles my mind because I can't fathom uploading 100 books a day, every day. But people do it. Ten is a good amount; 20 is doable in most cases. For me, that's where I stop. I've done it a few times, but it's certainly not common for me. Stay consistent and upload what you can every day, and in no time, you'll be rocking KDP.

Amazon has made a great change, limiting uploads to 1000 per week. Some people are using software to upload hundreds a day and this put a stop to them. I still think 1000 is too many. Why? Because it hurts you, me, and everyone else by taking up Amazon's time. They approve every cover personally. Someone is authorizing and rejecting them. It used to take about 24 hours to get approved; since that software came out, it's more like 3-5 days and more. I thought Amazon would smack that software down by now. I'm still holding out hope. I've checked it out, and to me, it seems black hat. I won't risk it.

Interiors

Too many people treat KDP and low and no content books like a hobby and not a business, if you treat it like a hobby then you will never make a "job income" from your books.

I personally treat KDP like a business because that's what it is, and because of this I have had some pretty great results over the last year and you can too if you start treating it like a real business! Just remember this...

"Your income will be in direct proportion to how much time and effort you put into running your business"

Another top tip is that you should focus on IPA's "Income Producing Activities" if you only focus on tasks that move your business forward then your business has no choice but to grow.

These IPA's are simple: Research - Create - Upload

If I don't do any research then I won't be able to create books and if I don't create books then I have nothing to upload, thus my business will not grow! so only focus on these tasks.

This can be every day, every other day or a day or two every week, it all depends on your situation, but it all comes down to staying consistent! Too many people give up before they have their breakthrough so if you really want to make this work then stick at it for 6 months to a year because you might not have your breakthrough until month 6.

Paddy of StackinProfit

kevinbarrymaguire.com/Printin-Profits

To make your interiors, you'll need either PowerPoint, Google Slides, Affinity Publisher (https://affinity.serif.com/en-gb/publisher), or Adobe InDesign. I recommend Affinity Publisher because it's a one-time fee and much faster than the first two options. They aren't paying me to say that, either. You can pay Microsoft or Adobe every month if you wish; it's up to you. Or Google Slides, that's free. You can use Canva too, but I don't recommend it with Slides being free and a better option.

The process is pretty much the same for each for the programs. Set your layout to 6x9 inches. If you're in Publisher, set it to only 1 page and add a master page. It's in the panel to the left. Do your work on the Master Page. Then you're going to leave about an inch to an inch and a half at the top of the page and draw a line across the page. Duplicate and drop the new line 8.7mm and repeat. I know Publisher has numbers that will pop up, telling you the distance between objects. I'm guessing InDesign does as well because Photoshop does. You can change the grid size in PowerPoint to 1/5 of an inch (no metrics, and I think that's close.) Otherwise, eyeball it or use a physical ruler.

You'll have to copy and paste each line unless you have Affinity Publisher, then you'll be done with the whole book in a matter of seconds. I'll explain that in a few. When you're done with the copy and paste, you're going to go to the panel on the left and copy the whole page, then paste until you have 110 pages.

With Publisher, you make your first line. Then right click on the layer in the Layers panel – on the right – and choose "Duplicate." Move it down the required 8.7mm. Then you type CTRL until the lines go to the bottom. Publisher knows you want a new line 8.7mm down from the previous line. It works with whatever you duplicate and move. It's an awesome feature in Publisher.

Now up on the top left of the left panel, you'll see three tabs: Pages, Assets, and Stock. You want to be on Pages. Then just down from there, you'll see Pages again. Two icons over to the right is, "Add more pages." In the box that pops up, change "Master Page" to B. Then add 109 pages. Done.

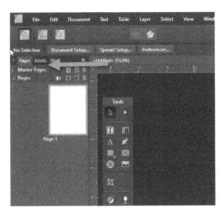

Figure 4-1

Figure 4-1 shows the Pages tab along with the Master Pages and Pages options. Master pages are awesome and are a feature in Adobe InDesign too. If you're going to have duplicate pages, you can designate the first one a Master (Master B) and do the work once. You can have multiple master pages in each project. And now you know one of the huge reasons I'm gung-ho on Affinity Publisher. (I haven't figured out how to duplicate Master A yet; it's always greyed out for me.)

No matter which software you use, this is easy work. It's work you only do once per no-content style too. There are times you'll want a customized interior, so you start with your template you just made, then add your customization. Don't forget to "Save As" and change the name. Keep your original template safe. The process is the same for all the no-content interiors. Only the lines change, sometimes drastically.

Other no-content options include: graph paper (large and small), dot grid, hexagon, isometric, story paper, sheet music, guitar tabs (popular!), shorthand, calligraphy, handwriting, Kanji practice, Cornell notes, sketch paper, comic book, and recipe. As you can see, the possibilities are endless. At the end of the book, I'll give you a chance to get some of these templates for free.

Dot grid paper is what is better known as bullet journal. But that term is trademarked, so we can't use it. Don't even try; it ain't worth losing your account over. Graph paper can be made in four squares per inch and five squares per inch.

Story paper is for kids to write short stories and draw a picture. You'll have a top line, made as handwriting paper, then a blank box to draw in, and more writing lines below. I'll have one of these templates in the free package at the end of the book. These should be 8.5x11 inches. Kids need lots of room!

Blank comic book pages are a big seller on Amazon, and I'll have these for you too. It's a bunch of blank boxes on a page. You'll want to offer several pages with different sizes on each page. Kind of like school photos, or even a comic book! Yep, just buy a comic book, and see how the pages are laid out. Then design your template in the same way.

For the rest, it's better that you look online for examples. Then create your own. Change up a little so you aren't plagiarizing. Amazon gets a lot of the same pages uploaded and will send you an email when they detect it. It will say something like "Do you have the rights to this book [title here]?" And a bunch of other words. I've received the email a few times. It looks scary, but they say if it is your work, to submit it again. Do that if it is your work, and it will get approved. If you used a template from someone else, also submit again. As long as you have permission, it's the same as it being your work. Mine will come with commercial rights, so you'll be ok.

Covers

Your covers can be as easy or complex as you like. They just need to look nice. No and low-content books are the only time you should make your own covers – unless you're a trained designer. If you're new to this, you can start with text only. Then start adding photos and illustrations.

I've only made covers with Adobe Photoshop and Affinity Designer. Those are the two I can give exact details on. The process is the same no matter what software you use, however. I know Patty of Stackin Profit has a very good, detailed course on low-content publishing, and he uses Canva for everything. As you'll remember, Canva is free software. You can get his course here (https://kevinbarrymaguire.com/stackin-profit) and get half off if you use my first name "Kevin" for the coupon code.

I have his course, and I also have his other course, the *LCB Vault*. That one is updated weekly; it's pretty awesome. You can get that one at the same link above, and the same coupon code applies. Both these courses are very detailed, and he doesn't keep any secrets. You will learn all he knows. All these links will be available at the end of the book, in a section titled, "Links." They will be spelled out there, just in case the links in the chapters don't work.

The first thing you want to do is head on over to Amazon and create a cover template. I usually just do a search for "KDP cover template," and it pops right up. You can also click this link, kdp.a-mazon.com/en_US/cover-templates, and save it to your favorites. It asks for the trim size, 6x9, 8.5x11, etc. Then page count, and finally, paper color. Every cover you make will need a new template if the page count, size, or color changes. If you keep everything the same, you can reuse your templates.

For color, I do it this way: If they're going to write in it, I choose white. If they're going to read it, then I choose cream. If you're making a book with color pages, choose color. So, all no and low-content books would have white paper. Cream paper is easier on the eyes, so my fiction and nonfiction are printed on cream. White is easier to write on.

So, now you've downloaded your template and unzipped it. I only unzip the .jpg file then delete the zip. I keep all templates in the same folder as the book folder. For journals, I keep everything the same and keep it in a separate folder. I like to keep things as fast and easy as possible

Right click on the template file and choose, "Open with Affinity Designer" or Photoshop, or whatever you're using. That's important. When you do it this way, you keep Amazon's exact proportions. If you open the software first, then try to make the dimensions, it gets messy – and slows you down. Nobody wants to work turtle slow; time really is money. Although, have you seen that video with the turtle sprinting? I felt like I'd been lied to my whole life. Those suckers are fast! So maybe nobody wants to be as slow as molasses. That's better. Molasses really is slow. But it makes for great barbecue sauce… and rum!

In both Photoshop and Designer, you can click on the rulers and drag down guidelines. I place a guideline at the edge of all the pink lines. That way, I know where all the borders are when my template is covered up. When I first started, I kept turning off layers and eyeballing my placement. It took months before I learned about the guidelines. They're a huge time-saver.

Figure 4-2

In figure 4-2, I show the template with gridlines, though they are hard to see here. They show better in figure 4-3. The arrow points to the ruler; not shown is the ruler to the left. Click inside the rulers to drag out the gridlines, light blue in both programs. I put one on the pink inside edges of the top, bottom, left, and right. I put more on both sides of the pink binder lines. You can't put any text or images in any of the pink areas. Your cover will get rejected if you do. It helps to click Ctrl plus the + key four or five times to zoom in. You can see the edges better and align them better. Click Ctrl+0 (zero) to get back to normal size.

If you will be writing on the back cover, it's a good idea to put gridlines on the top and bottom edges of the yellow barcode box. You can't have any text or images in that space either.

Figure 4-3

You can see the gridlines much better on the black background. This is what I normally do for no-content books – a black background. Why? Because a lot of my no-content books start off as t-shirt designs. Then I transfer the design to the front cover (right side.) As I've mentioned, I design all my t-shirts on a black background. It sells the most. If my no or low-content books start off without a t-shirt design, then the color *might* change. There are times when black wouldn't be good, like notebooks and journals for Valentine's Day, Christmas, or just about any other holiday.

To get the colored box in Designer, just click the rectangle tool and draw the box from the top left corner down to the bottom right corner. Now change the color to whatever you want, then turn off the template layer. I usually delete the template layer at this point. I don't need it anymore; the guidelines tell me everything I need to know.

To get the cover color in Photoshop, click "Layers" in the top menu, then "New Fill Layer." Drag your box over the template, then follow the prompts the rest of the way. I think there is one more step before choosing the color. It's been a while since I've used it.

The left side is the back cover and for no and low-content books, I leave it blank about 70% of the time. If a notebook is for kids, I'll add a name box on the back so they can use it for school. The right side is the front cover and the small section in the middle is the spine. That's where you put your spine text – just the title for these books.

Amazon requires your title on the front cover or the spine. To keep your covers pretty, use the spine. This is another reason to use 110 pages versus 100. Amazon requires 100 pages minimum to add spine text, and I've tried it. The text is too small for most people to read and sometimes gets rejected. At 110 pages, I use a size 9 font with Calibri font, and it works every time. I get my title and subtitle on the spine and leave my cover either text free or with other, more appropriate text.

If you do publish books with fewer pages – like coloring books and children's books, there is some good news. Only the title must be on the cover. The subtitle does not need to appear anywhere except the book listing and title page. So that's cool. Keep your title short and pretty. Put everything else in the subtitle.

I can't get into the how-to's of the software you're using. It would be a book in itself. Affinity has a video tutorial page for each software on their website. I think Adobe does too. You can also find lots of videos on YouTube to learn your software. Another great place to learn software and just about anything else, is Udemy (https://kevinbarrymaguire.com/Udemy.) I use them for everything, and it's how I learned to use Affinity Photo and Designer. There isn't a class for Publisher yet.

The rest is just adding your cover text and design. The first few took me a while, but once I got used to what I was doing I got much faster. I can whip out covers lickety-split now. T-shirt designs too. Man, I was scary with those in the beginning! Slow and bad designs. It's all part of the learning process though. I'm much better with those now too.

One thing you can do with your back cover if you have a nice photo or illustration on your front cover is to wrap it around the book. Place the image on the front cover, then put the image on the back cover too. Make them meet in the middle. Now flip the image on the back cover horizontally. On Designer, there is a button on the top to flip horizontally. In Photoshop, it's under the edit or image menu. When you stop paying Adobe, you don't have Photoshop anymore, so I can't check.

I planned to show you good covers and bad covers here, but as I was looking at covers on Amazon, it occurred to me that the covers are copywrite protected, and I shouldn't use them in my book. So I'll ask, what makes a good cover?

Start with a good, clean, and thick font. You can get free fonts from.fontsquirrel.com, but make sure you're choosing ones with commercial use rights. Creative Fabrica gives away one free font per day, with commercial use rights - https://kevinbarry-maguire.com/creative-fabrica. I have an account with them and get unlimited fonts, images, and crafts from their website. It's just one monthly fee for all of it. It's perfect for what I do with print on demand (POD.) The link will take you to the subscription page, but you can order singles too, or just check out the free stuff.

Most of the time, you will want to put an image on the cover. There are lots of journals with text only, and it's a great way to start. Simple sells. Most of the images you use will be illustrations. You can use photographs too, but rarely. I'd really only use them for plants and animals. But there are exceptions to every rule.

Figure 4-4

Since I couldn't include real covers in this book, I made a sample and can walk you through it. In figure 4-4, you'll notice I used white again when I clearly said I almost always use black. Good call, you're paying attention. I like that. I started out with a black cover, but when I put the guidelines on, my photographer training kicked in. I've been a photographer since the film days. I've processed film and paper and was a darkroom master.

I started my photographer life in 1988 when I was 19 years old. So about ten-ish years before digital took over. I could see that image in black and white, and I knew it wasn't going to work. The paperback version of this book will have black and white photos; you understand why by now. Most e-readers will also show black and white photos. The guidelines would be invisible on the black background.

When designing, start with the center and move out. I placed the image first. I bought this image from Deposit Photos, so I'm allowed to use it here. There is something else, try not to use free photo sites. Some of those photos may not have been uploaded by the photographer or artist and so you won't have the real rights to use the photo. I have the rights to use the fonts as well. The top one is called, "Beer Font," and the bottom one is, "Blauer." Both from Creative Fabrica.

Placing the photo was easy, the curved text is a little tricky. I suggest you go to YouTube and search "text on a path" for the software you're using. You'll sell more books, shirts, anything else when you use curved text. Most people aren't using it, so it sets you apart, and it looks better.

I also chose curved text because of the moon. It's already round, so I continued up with a round shape. It's more pleasing to the eye to keep the same shapes. Straight text there would take the serenity right out of the photo.

You'll notice the bottom of the drawing is straight, and so is my text. For the spine text – the title and subtitle – I start with a larger font on the back cover. I type what I need while being able to see it, then I change it to size 9 (Calibri, remember) and rotate it. A trick with Photoshop and Designer is to hold shift while you rotate. It moves the text in 15-degree angles and will give you a perfect up and down. If you don't hold shift, it will take a long time to get it right.

Then I move it over to the center and get it close to vertical center. Next, I enlarge the cover so I can see the text and borders clearly. Then get the vertical center right – you'll see a green or red line, telling you it's centered – depending on the software. Then I worry about horizontal center. That's a green line.

Done! It's that easy. You can make it more or less complicated, but that's the general process. Try to keep it as simple as you can. Remember KISS – Keep It Simple Silly. I learned it with a different word other than silly. But we'll just leave it at that.

Bonus tips:

1. Don't use more than four colors in any design – KDP, Merch, or anything else.
2. You shouldn't use more than two fonts in any design.
3. Learn the rule of thirds – it's all over YouTube. It will help your composition.
4. Have fun. This can be the most fun job you've ever had; roll with it.

Again, there are exceptions to every rule, it's ok to break rules sometimes. I see it a lot when doing my research. Use your best judgement.

Uploading

Now you're ready to start uploading your first no-content notebook. If you don't have one already, open a KDP account at www.kdp.amazon.com . It's pretty easy and doesn't take too long. Good news, there are no country restrictions that I know of. There are people in Facebook groups from all over the world uploading all kinds of books to Amazon.

When you're all set up, go back to www.kdp.amazon.com and make sure you're on the "Bookshelf" tab at the top. Under that, you'll see, "Create a New Title" and eBook and Paperback options. Choose Paperback, and you'll be taken to the Paperback Details page. Language, title, and subtitle are self-explanatory. You're all rock stars, and you did your homework, so you're ready to rip.

Series is very rare in the no and low-content world. It's most used in fiction when you have a three, four, or more book series. It can happen in nonfiction too, but that's also rare. Edition number is the same, very rare in this world. That's more a nonfiction thing, especially for history and medical type books.

Author. That's rarely you. It's your book, but you're not going to put your real name there in most cases. I would have preferred a pen name for this book, but nobody would know who I am and wouldn't care about anything I wrote. The problem I have is my name is common in Ireland and there are a lot of famous Kevin Maguire's. I'm not one of them, yet! I'm not the comic book writer, or the journalist, or the artist. I'm just me, Kevin Maguire from Steilacoom, WA. Born to Eugene Maguire of Belfast, N Ireland.

I guess my mother had something to do with it too. She was

born in the USA. One of the funniest 1-star reviews I got in my *Aftermath* series (we all get them, and I don't fret about them anymore) was a guy saying I wasn't real. I'm pretty sure I am! I'm in the Steilacoom HS yearbooks from the graduating years of 1984-1987. I'm the dork that looks like George Michael. Shh. It was the 80s. I apologize for nothing!

Figure 4-5

There I am in figure 4-5. That is a yearbook photo from my senior year. A few weeks later I added a cast to my other arm. A few months later, a knee brace. I was in a cast of some sort a lot. I played hard. I liked that shirt.

Where were we? Pen names! If you're smart about it, you can use a keyword as a pen name. I've heard people say they had some pen names refused, but it doesn't hurt to try. Something like "Jenny's Journals" can work, just check to make sure it isn't used already. Then check uspto.com to make sure there are no trademarks. You're going to get oh-so familiar with that website; bookmark it. They don't make this process easy and haven't updated their website since 1996. I can't confirm that, but you'll see what I mean. From there, click on the box, "Search our trademark database (TESS.)" Now click the first selection under "Select A Search Option." It says, "Basic Word Mark Search (New User)" and you're finally at the screen you need to be.

After all that work to get there, you're on a timer. I've never timed it, but when it runs out, you have to start all over again, from the first screen. On the current screen, type "Jenny's Journals" into the search box and click "Submit Query" or hit enter. It says no records were found, so it can be used, as long as nobody else is using it. We'll get more into that in the Merch chapter, where you'll be using the trademark check for every design and every listing.

Contributors can almost always be left blank too. That would be for fiction and nonfiction if you have co-authors, illustrators, editors you'd like to give credit to, etc. if you need it; it's also self-explanatory.

Now the description. This is the most important box to get the sale. The cover gets their attention, the description gets the sale or sends your would-be customer looking elsewhere. This is so important, I'm devoting a whole chapter to it – Chapter 8 Writing Copy. For no and low-content books, it's pretty straightforward. Although, for self-help type low-content journals, you can step up your game and knock out the competition with a good description.

I'm going to show you the description for one of my notebooks. Almost everything is the same for every notebook I upload. I change the title and design description and that's it. This is only for notebooks and other no-content books.

My Body Is My Journal Tattoo Body Art Quote Notebook and Diary

Design features text saying, "My body is my journal. Tattoos are my story." Your tattooed friends will love it! Great for taking notes, writing notes and poems, lists, passwords, or anything else you can think of. Use it as a diary or journal. Whatever floats your boat.

Makes an excellent gift idea for birthdays, Christmas, back to school, or any special occasion

Features include:

- *6 x 9 Inches*
- *110 Pages*
- *College Ruled*
- *Perfect size to carry around*

Use it to keep your notes, a diary, and even a journal.

*Scroll up and click **"Buy Now"** to get yours!*

Ignore the italics, it's part of Word's quote box feature. You'll notice the title is bold and larger print. That's to call attention to your description; it catches the eye, and it's what you want. I've also got other parts bolded; that's to keep the eyes from getting bored. It's the same reason you put blank lines between paragraphs. It's also a good idea to keep your paragraphs short. Otherwise, people will think "tldr." That means, "Too long, didn't read," and it will kill your sales.

You always want a bulleted list in your descriptions. People are busy or have short attentions spans. They don't want to read long descriptions; give those people what they want. You need them; they don't need you. They have options, and you want to be that option. The last line is important and should be in all your book descriptions.

Studies have shown that you get more sales with a call to action – i.e., the "buy now." Some people feel weird adding that line. Don't. It's all about making the sale and that will help you make the sale. People want to be told what to do, so tell them… buy now!

You'll notice a lot of descriptions on Amazon that aren't formatted. It's plain, boring text from start to finish. The sellers either don't know html is available to them, or don't know how to code it. Lucky for me, I do. Luckier for me and you, there are good people who have Amazon description editors for us to use, free! It's much faster than coding by hand, trust me.

Dave Chesson has a good one on his Kindlepreneur website, https://kevinbarrymaguire.com/Book-Description. It is easy to use and will help make your descriptions snap off the page. I suggest using it for every book description. Formatted text will increase your sales.

Publishing Rights should be an easy answer for you. If you wrote it, created it, or paid someone to write or create it, you have the publishing rights. If it's public domain work, say so. You are able to publish public domain works, but I haven't done it and never looked into it. So, I can't tell you the rules. I have heard it can be lucrative, however.

Now you need to enter all those keywords you found. You get seven boxes with 50 characters each. You know how to fill these boxes now, so I don't need to repeat the process. Use every box.

Categories will help get your books seen. For these books, just choose two that are close to your genre, or topic. If you see, "General," don't use it. Your book will have a hard time getting seen. You want your categories to be relevant, just like your keywords. But don't fret over it for no-content.

Adult content. For no-content journals and notebooks, I don't see how you could ever check, "Yes." Covers aren't allowed nudity and "side boob" will get your book placed in the Amazon dungeon, never to be seen by anyone. "Hand bras" are the same. Don't do it. The only time you'll really ever check "Yes" is if you've written erotica. Romance with a little sex can usually get by with clicking "no." When you click "yes," you will not be able to advertise the book on Amazon. It's a crushing blow. Click "Save and Continue" on the bottom right.

Print ISBN. An ISBN is an International Standard Book Number and is used by bookstores to find your book. They will not look for Amazon ISBNs, however. For no and low-content books, let Amazon assign a free ISBN. A single ISBN costs $125, so free is pretty good. You can buy them in blocks and get them cheaper. I bought a block of 100 for books that I write or have ghost-written. Those 100 cost me $575, but it's worth it when you're writing your own books.

Publication Date: Leave it empty and let Amazon fill it out.

Print options are self-explanatory. Choose your paper color, size, bleed, and cover style. Bleed is something I haven't mentioned yet because lined notebooks always use bleed. It means your content goes to the edge of the page. Without bleed, it stops on an invisible margin. That will be explained later.

The manuscript is the interior. In this case, the pdf with the lined pages you made. You can upload in other formats, .docx, for example. But for these, it's best to use a pdf. Your paperback cover will always be a pdf while an eBook cover will be a .jpg.

After your pdfs are uploaded, you can click "Launch Previewer" under Book Review. Make some coffee first, or take a bath, walk the dog. Anything to kill time while Amazon is uploading and scanning your documents. They're scanning for spelling errors, copyright info, plagiarism, etc. When you finally get to look at the previewer, make sure the cover looks nice, then check out the pages. I only look at two pages for no-content, because they're all the same. Save and continue.

Now you're on the pricing page, or how much do you want to get paid? The first box is "Territories." You should always be checking "All territories." Then "Pricing and Royalty" is next. There is a box to enter your price. I price all my no-content at $6.99, and it gets me a $2.02 royalty per sale. There are those who like to undercut that price, let them. I'm not working for under $2.

They will pick up a few sales from people looking for the lowest price. Who cares? Most people look at the lowest price and think "lowest quality" and won't buy it. Take pride in yourself and have confidence in your product. Don't feel the need to charge less than $6.99.

Under the pricing box, you'll see "Expanded Distribution" and a checkbox. If you check it, your notebook will be available off Amazon, at a cost. Amazon will send your book to Ingram Spark to distribute elsewhere, and they take a hefty cut. Your $2.02 royalty goes down to 63 cents. Much lower than my $2 minimum. Do it anyway. Remember, every rule has an exception.

You'll be getting paid less per sale, but you'll be making more sales. It's extra money that shows up sometime during the third week of the month. On your KDP dashboard, you'll see a "reports" tab. That's where all your sales show up. Paperback is gray, eBooks are yellow, and expanded distribution is red. I think of it as bonus money.

Under that are the 7 other marketplaces. The UK is in pounds, all the European countries are in euros, Japan in yen, and Canada in their dollar. I never leave them at Amazon's suggestion because the pricing looks crazy. There is a reason people use "99" for pricing. People like it. They buy it. I've been reading that "97" works well too. Sometimes that isn't doable on the foreign currencies, however. You don't want to raise the price too high or make it too low. So I use "49" instead.

For no-content, I charge 5.59 pounds for the UK, 6.49 euros for the European countries, 999 yen, and $8.99 Canadian. The Japanese price is much higher than Amazon suggests because I've read Amazon doesn't calculate the price correctly, and the authors lose money.

Next are the "Terms & Conditions" and a request for a proof copy. A proof copy is your notebook with a band across the front and back cover saying, "Proof Copy" or something close. I've never ordered one myself. I've only seen them on YouTube. The purpose is so you can see if there are any errors and that everything looks the way you want it to look.

Author copies are better because they don't have the band

across the cover and are still discounted. You can buy author copies and sell them on your own, though I'm not sure I'd do that with notebooks.

Next, you click that orange button that says, "Publish Your Paperback Book." You did it! In a few days, your notebook will be live on Amazon. Congratulations! Now rinse and repeat the process with as many keywords as you can find.

Type "panda notebooks" in the Amazon search and see what pops up. Take note of what is selling and make something similar. Similar. Don't copy. Then do your keyword research and sell more books.

My friend Dale L Roberts just made a new and detailed video on how to upload, check it out here: bit.ly/Dales-Upload.

Low-Content Niches

ALWAYS be trying to improve on every aspect of this business. I started low content book publishing November 2018, I had no design skills and no previous experience with publishing, but I had the willingness to constantly be improving and always getting better at designing and research and it slowly paid off! (I still learn and get better every day)

So, to recap:

Create books around what people are searching for.

Treat LCB like a business and stay consistent.

Always try to be improving.

Paddy of StackinProfit

kevinbarrymaguire.com/Printin-Profits

According to dictionary.com, a niche is "a distinct segment of a market." That's the definition pertaining to us, anyway. If you're researching "werebear shapeshifter romance," that's a niche. If you're searching gaslight romance, that's a niche. Mother's Day is a niche, as is Father's Day. I think you understand now.

I'm going to give you a short list of niches to get you started. The first two I named above are niches, but I'm not sure they would do well for no-content. But then, I've never researched it. The savvy entrepreneur might go ahead and research that too.

- Tea
- Wine*
- Coffee*
- Pizza
- Cheese
- Cupcake
- Bacon*
- Banana
- Snake
- Dog*
- Cat*
- Pug
- Pig
- Hamster
- Bowling
- Running
- Nurse*
- Manager
- Juicing
- Mermaid
- Heart
- Space* $
- Planet
- Fox

- Zebra
- Knitting
- Baseball*
- Fishing*
- Strawberry $
- Hedgehog
- Astrology* $
- Flowers
- Avocado*

(This is a small part of a large list I got from the Printin Profits course.)

I know you're wondering what the asterisk and dollar signs mean, so I'll tell you. I'm a nice guy that way. The asterisks are showing hard niches, lots of competition to the point of being over-saturated. The dollar sign means I have shirts in that niche making money.

So just because a niche has a lot of competition, doesn't mean you need to back off. It means it's going to be a fight, and you're going to have to work for it. You need better ideas and better designs than what is available.

Another way to break into a tough niche is to combine it with another niche that isn't so tough. "Wine and reading," or "Nurses who love zebras." Cliché alert: Think outside the box. There are thousands of niches out there; just about anything you do or like is a niche. Your hobbies are niches, animals, plants, and flowers are niches.

Animal is a niche, alligator is a subniche. Engineer is a niche (and a big one) but electrical engineer is a subniche. Break things down to their smallest part and tackle those niches.

. . .

Chapter 4 Exercises, Part I

Wait, what? Part I means there will be a "Part II," right? Right. A little extra homework never killed anyone, and this chapter is much bigger than I anticipated – over 8,000 words already!

I've gone into great detail on how to create a no-content book. You've done the research already, now put it to use. Either make your interior or use one I will make available to you by signing up to my email list - https://kevinbarrymaguire.com/POD-Signup. Then make your cover. Remember, you can use only text, and if you're new to making graphics, that's the easiest way to start.

If you haven't yet, sign up for an account at www.kdp.amazon.com and upload the book. Get the first one out of the way and work out any kinks you might have. But get it done, and you'll be ahead of the "I'll do it tomorrow" people.

Most of all, have fun. This is fun "work."

Note:

Between the time I wrote this chapter and now, Amazon made a few changes. They are giving priority to "real books" during the approval process. That means lined notebooks, and a few others are taking several weeks to get approved. Keep chugging, keep uploading. They still sell and still make money.

Build yourself a solid base of notebooks, then move on to journals. Notebooks are easier and will train you for the process. It's great training.

Low-Content Books

DOS:

---

*Dos:*1. Do your research 1st - before you spend your time working on an interior, do your research to ensure there's a demand for it

2. Start at home - when you first start out, it's best to focus on topics/themes that you're familiar with and have a passion for. Some of the best interiors are built from necessity. If you know the topic, you're more likely to create something that resonates with the ideal audience.

3. Check out the competition - check out the books on the market similar to what you want to do. Check out their reviews. (good reviews show you what to include in your book, negative reviews show you what you can do to make your book *BETTER* than the competition.

4. KISS - Keep It Super Simple - for your first few interiors, focus on the process and dialing things in. I'm not saying put our garbage, but don't spend weeks trying to perfect your interior. (Done is better than perfect)

DON'TS:

---

*Don'ts:*1. Don't go too deep - don't create dozens of books in the same niche, until you've had proven sales

2. Don't copy your competitors - use your competition as a starting point and inspiration. Your goal is to make something better.

3. Don't copy yourself - once you have a book/interior that sells, that doesn't mean make 100 more books the same but with different covers/sizes. Take what's selling and find ways to make it better. (i.e.

vary the interior, read your reviews and see what can be added/removed, based on customer feedback)

4. Don't compare yourself - everyone's journey and situation is different. It's real easy to look at where others are at in their business and try to compare yourself. DON'T! The only person you should compare yourself to is...you! Compare your sales month over month, year over year. If you're seeing progress, then you're succeeding. If you don't see progress, investigate.(what changed, what's holding you back, should you run ads, etc.)

BONUS TIP: *Enjoy the ride - life's too short to not enjoy what you're doing. If you're not having fun, then consider taking a break.*

Keith Wheeler YouTube

bit.ly/Keith-YT

Low-content books are similar to no-content but will make you more money if you put quality over quantity. It's still a numbers game, but you can charge more for journals than you can for notebooks and such. Why? Because it takes more work, and people will pay more for a journal than they will a notebook. I have several I sell for $9.99, and people tell me they have higher priced journals. I think that's pretty awesome.

To determine your price, look at the journals in your niche and see what they're selling for. Stay in that range. That is how you determine the size of your journal as well. There are two typical sizes for journals, 6x9 and 8.5x11. Use whatever is most common already in the niche. It's common because that's what people want.

There are times you may want to do it differently. Kelly Roberts has said she looked at a niche and decided to try a different size. It worked. I wouldn't make a habit of it, but if it looks right, try it. You never know. Here YouTube channel: youtube.com/kellipublish.

There are many types of low-content books, from planners to journals and coloring books to puzzle books. "Low" means you aren't writing anything, or just a few words, but it's more involved than a no-content book. These are more than just endless lined pages. You're going to put in a little extra work for that extra money. It's a fair trade.

Planners are good sellers, but everyone knows that, and it's got a lot of competition now. I only sold a handful for 2020 so far and most people have bought their 2020 planners by now – now being February 15, 2020. I don't think I'll make any for 2021. I have more profitable options to take on. Should you attempt it, they should be uploaded by October 2020 to take full advantage of Quarter 4.

What is quarter 4, you ask? It's Q4, the most profitable quarter of the year! It's where a lot of your sales will come, record months. In a word, it's pure awesome. Topped with awesome so hot, the sun says, "Damn, son! That's hot!" Always be working toward Q4. October, November, December.

Coloring books still do well but can be expensive to make if you can't draw. Another option is to search "coloring pages" on Creative Fabrica and see what comes up for your niche. That would be the cheapest way. I've found some at Deposit Photos too.

The problem with using those sites is other people may have used some of the images you chose. You will not be able to say, "Original designs." Some people may notice they've seen the designs before – and comment about it in a review. I've seen them. I do use those sites for my coloring books and haven't got those comments yet. One reason is Creative Fabrica is still very new to everyone, so there aren't many of their designs out there.

The next way is to hire an illustrator. That is expensive, and I don't recommend it unless you're sure of your keyword research and have more money to spend on ads. You'll need 20-25 images, plus the cover image. The cover is one of those images colored in. You can add the text later or have the illustrator do it. I do my own text. The cover image is just that, an image. You still have to place it on the paperback template.

You can use Upwork to find an illustrator and pay gobs of money, and it would be worth it. You can go to fiverr.com and pay a smaller gob of money too. I'd be careful there though. But I don't go to either of them. I use workana.com to find artists.

Why? Because you can find quality artists at a less expensive price. Basic economics. Most of the artists are from South America, but they've recently opened up world-wide.

Workana has their scammers though, so you must be careful. Do not pay until you check every image via a Google Image search. That's how I found out an artist I chose wasn't an artist at all. He was a no good, rotten scoundrel. A yellow bellied, piece of crap, lousy scammer. Put in your ad that you will make sure all images are originals.

Workana has an English version of the site, for those of us who don't understand Spanish. The website is easy to use and navigate. I don't foresee any issues there.

Puzzle books are money in the bank. The thing with these books is people always need more. When they finish one, they can't just start over, they need a new one, a different one. You can search Amazon for puzzle books and see all the different ones you can make.

There is the hot selling Sudoku, mazes, word search, crosswords, and many others. You can mix them up too; those are called, "activity books." Then you can add tic tac toe, hangman, and more. You can even add coloring pages. The sky is the limit for an activity book!

If you want a great course to teach you all about low-content, I suggest Low-Content Domination - https://kevinbarry-maguire.com/Low-Content. I took that course, and it helped me increase my income. The teaching doesn't end when the course is finished. There is a private Facebook group you can join when you purchase the course. Gerald is there to answer any questions you may have. You'll also get help from me and other members. It's a good group.

Between no-content and low-content, this is where the money is at. I suggest doing some no-content first. It will help you get the process down, and you'll learn to speed up the process along the way. Get yourself a few hundred, at least. I still do both; no-content makes money. If the money is there, so am I!

You can get mazes made from Fiverr gigs for a decent price. Maze books do very well on Amazon. I use Simply Maze Crazy, however - https://kevinbarrymaguire.com/Maze-Crazy. It's a software you pay for once and use over and over again. If you use my affiliate link, you will get $5 off the purchase price.

For crosswords, I use Armored Penguin's crossword maker - kevinbarrymaguire.com/crossword. It's really good, easy to use, free, and commercial use is allowed. When you find free puzzle software, always check for commercial use rights. Most do not have them. Believe me, I've spent hours looking. The only one I found that does, I just told you about.

Some niches you want to pay attention to are any you can add "for kids" or "for adults" to. You can even throw in "for teens." That works well too. So, type in something like, "crossword puzzles for teens" and see where that takes you.

Marketing

The only marketing I do for no-content books are Amazon Ads. I set the per click price at around 12-20 cents and limit them to $5 per day. Breathe. It's ok. Amazon almost never comes near the $5, and never has for me on a no or low-content book.

Two Christmases ago, I had one book max out every day for almost an entire month. It's ok because that was a nonfiction book making me over $50 per day. I will trade $5 for $50 every time. Without those ads, my book would have been lost to the competition. It was in a very competitive keyword – the Keto Diet. That ad still runs today but isn't even costing me $5 a month.

There is more you can do with low-content books. A lot of people run Facebook groups to sell their low-content books. I know a few people who own groups for coloring books. There are groups for just about every kind of journal. If you get 10,000 people in a Facebook group, and you release a new book, you could get at least 200 sales every time you release a book and make a post about it.

How did I reach that number? At any given time, 2% of the people seeing your post, will purchase. I got that information from watching Dan Brock on YouTube. He's all about using YouTube to make money, and the numbers apply to links in video descriptions. I think it would be higher for a group post, but I'll keep it at 2%.

Here's the kicker, when Amazon sees all those sales in a short amount of time, they're going to start promoting your book for you. You'll end up in emails and show up on more screens. Of course, your ranking will skyrocket too. The more people who see your book, the more that buy.

The Facebook group jumpstarts your success. What's our favorite F word? You guessed it - Facebook groups are free! If you have an email list to promote to at the same time, you're in business!

The only other marketing I do for low content is Pinterest. I've been thinking about using YouTube too, but so far, I only use YouTube for my fiction books and one nonfiction. If you don't have a Pinterest account, you should make one.

Make a pin with your book cover on it and fancy, inspiring words that people love to read but not follow, and boom! You have a pin. Create a board around the niche, fill it with pins from other people, and your book pins. One board for each niche – you want targeted traffic.

We'll dive into YouTube marketing later. But for now, if you don't have a YouTube account, it's 2020 and about time you caught up with the rest of us. I have five of them. If your personal account is full of questionable videos, make another account. You can add an account to your current one, search it on Google, or better yet, DuckDuckGo. That's all I use now. The Duck doesn't spy on us. The Duck has morals.

Low-Content Courses:

Stackin Profit (and vault): kevinbarrymaguire.com/stackin-profit

Low-content Domination: kevinbarrymaguire.com/Low-Content.

Writing Fiction

Building a fan base is key. Grow your audience and consider building your e-mail list gradually with paid traffic.
Jacob Rothenberg, Publishing Evolution
kevinbarrymaguire.com/Publishing-Evolution

Some of you are going to tune out here, but you hold on just a dern minute. This may interest you too. You don't have to write a 50,000-word novel to write fiction. You can, of course. But Amazon has what are called "Short Reads," and they start at 15 minutes. Those books are 15 minutes and under. Then it goes to 30, 45, 60, 90, and two hours.

Amazon bills these as "Great stories in one sitting." People like them. Everyone has an imagination. Some use it better than others. I'm talking to you, Steven King, but we all have one. Can you start and finish a story in 1-11 pages? That's a 15-minute short read. If you can write 12-21 pages, you've got a 30-minute short read.

A 45-minute short read is 22-32, and a one-hour short read is 33-43 pages. A 90-minute read will take 44-64 pages, and the two-hour one will require 65-100 pages. Those are a bit more involved but still not a novel.

You can charge 99 cents for each short read – avoid calling them books, a mistake I'll tell you about in a few minutes. Amazon won't let you go below 99 cents, except to offer if free. They don't like that but will do it IF your book is offered else-where for free. We're not going to do that though.

Our short reads will be entered into KDP Select and let people who are entered, read for free. Then Amazon will pay us per page read. A page read is worth 0.0045 cents, on average (it changes month to month.) Get off the ceiling. It's not that excit-ing, calm down. Ok, it's not much by itself, but when you have an army of short reads pulling in page reads, it adds up. Or if you have a longer book, it will add faster.

Why would you want to avoid calling your short read a book? Because I did it on my first one. It went to #1 in multiple cate-gories. I knocked THE John Grisham out of the #1 spot to do it.

Figure 4-6

I snapped this screenshot sometime after passing Mr. Grisham. I wish I would have got it with him still #2, but I did get him in front of me.

Figure 4-7

As you can see in figure 4-7, I was excited just to be second to John Grisham. I never dreamed I'd pass him. But I did. And that's the beauty of self-publishing – you can too.

But why was calling it a "book" a mistake? The subtitle here was *"Book 1 It Has Begun."* I thought people understood they were buying a short read. The categories all said "short read" in them. The book details said 43 pages. Everyone reads all the information before buying, right? Wrong.

Oh boy, was I ever wrong. The book has lots of good reviews and a healthy amount of bad ones. About 99% of the bad reviews say something similar to, "Too short." A lot say, "Book? More like a chapter!"

Bad reviews are good. What? Yes, they're good… if you use them correctly. People are giving you solid information on what they didn't like. And there was that one who told me I wasn't a real person. He's an oddball; you'll get those. If you use that information to write your next book, it will be a better book.

My next book was longer but still got the "too short" reviews.

So, the third one was even longer but still too short. Whew. I bundled the three and sell them as a bundle. I don't get the "too short" reviews on that one. I also added a few bonus chapters about how the male and female leads met.

Book four was much longer at 55,000 words. Not short!

I also learned not to make paperback versions of short reads. Man, were people pissed off! "A pamphlet, not a book!" Ouch. Amazon combines the paperback and eBook reviews, and the worst reviews came from paperback buyers. I have removed those from Amazon, but the reviews remain. It sucks. That was a hard lesson.

So, short reads: Good. Easy. Do not call them books. Do not make a paperback version. I just saved you a lot of heartache and bad reviews.

A note on pricing. When my first book started climbing the charts, it was priced at 99 cents and was getting a lot of page reads. I was making $20 a day on page reads alone during that time. On a short read – it is an 8900 word "book." I tried something and changed the price to $2.99, and my sales skyrocketed. Instead of making about 35 cents per sale, I was now making $2 per sale, and my income also skyrocketed.

I put a lot of that money back into my business and hired a ghost writer company to write a few nonfiction books for me. Those are under super-secret pen names. I won't divulge them. I gotta protect my keywords there. I'll talk about ghost writers later.

What will you write about? Everyone says, "Write what you know." So that's what I did. I know preppers and prepping. I know how to survive in the wild. I worked Intelligence in the Navy and know a thing or two there. That's where the enemies come from. You already know I'm getting back into short reads with a new series that will also be about a prepper, in the post-apocalyptic niche. I also read a lot – a lot – of post-apocalyptic fiction.

What do you know? Can you turn it into a story? How about a series of short stories? Here's the thing, if you can think it, you can write it. All that daydreaming you do? Write it down. You need at least one character, a goal, at least one conflict, then resolution. The more conflict, the better the story can be. Your main character can have some internal struggles (conflict) while fighting an external conflict. Make it interesting. Your character should never be a superhero, unless he is a superhero, of course. But then you're probably writing a comic.

KDP Select

Not every book you publish will make money. If you have a bad release, don't give up. Learn from your mistakes and your next book will be a hit.

Jacob Rothenberg, *Publishing Evolution*
kevinbarrymaguire.com/Publishing-Evolution

When to use it? When to stay out?

KDP Select is where your page reads come from. During the upload process, you'll see the option to join KDP Select. If you choose to do so, you may not offer your book anywhere else; your book must remain exclusive to Amazon – and they check. If your book is available elsewhere and you're in Select, the result can be disastrous.

A benefit to page reads is every download of your book will increase your ranking. So, you're getting paid per page, plus you get a higher rank. I'd suggest putting every book in Select for at least the first 90-Day period. You can select the opt out button at any time, and it will keep you in until the 90 days are up.

Nonfiction is a little different. They don't really make money in KDP Select. You'll get the ranking boost, which is huge, but the page reads aren't there. It seems people read only the sections they're interested in and no more.

You can enter your nonfiction book into KDP Select and then email KDP to withdraw early if it isn't working out for you. Understand, you will lose any page read money you earned for that book when you leave early. I've done it a few times and have not regretted it.

Editing

Before you upload a book, you must have someone edit it. Someone not being you. You will be the first editor, then write the second draft. Someone else needs to see it after you. If you can't afford an editor (again, there are some good ones on Fiverr,) then have a friend, spouse, parent, anyone you can trust, read and edit it. By trust, I mean they paid attention in English class.

Someone who knows the difference between there, their, and they're. Someone who knows if you used to, too and two correctly. You'll be surprised how many mistakes you'll make, even when you know the difference in the words. Sometimes autocorrect will burn you.

My worst mistake was a killer. It was in book 4 of my *Aftermath* series. One reason I like short stories is I'm disabled. I have a bum shoulder, and typing for long periods hurts. So, to answer the demand of the readers and make a longer book, I got Dragon Naturally Speaking. I spoke the entire novel.

I understood Dragon would type some words wrong, and I kept a list of those words for when I finished. Then I did a "find and replace" for each instance. But I missed one. My editor missed it too. It was a nightmare when I found out. I had some deer in the book and mentioned "deer" four times. Only, Dragon spelled "dear" all four times. The very first review mentioned it. She was kind and gave me four stars. Others weren't so kind. It took a few days to get the fix approved. That hurt.

If you're going to use speech to text software, you need good eyes on the paper. Word has a "Read Aloud" tool on the Review tab; it's on the left side. I use that when I'm done writing. I make Word read the whole book to me. When doing so, you can hear wrong word usage – Word's spellcheck won't alert you to wrong words because they're spelled correctly.

It will also alert you to run-on sentences. You know, those sentences that go on and on forever without a break for the reader because you're so excited to get the information out that you forget all about proper English and just keep writing and writing because you have words, great words, you have the best words and people need to hear them now! Whew. Kind of like that.

I'm almost always reading along too. I must have been talking to my wife or daughter while listening to that chapter, because I didn't notice. It is something I will be more careful about moving forward. It was a costly mistake. Reviews don't go away because you fixed the error.

Just like bad reviews, mistakes are good if you learn from them. I goofed. I must pay better attention when dictating and doing my self-edit. Even though I had an editor, I'm not going to blame him. It's my book, my responsibility. Editors are human, believe it or not. Mistakes happen. You still need to hire one – or ask a trusted friend or family member.

Those extra eyes will catch things you miss over and over again. You'll see. Your brain knows what the words say or are *supposed* to say. Therefore, you skip right over easy mistakes. Even when you do your first edit, you should put the manuscript away for a few weeks. Give yourself time to forget some things. That will help you catch things but not everything. Editors make writing suggestions too. So they save you in more ways than one.

. . .

Beginner Writing Tips

1. Start off with a bang. Don't bore readers with background information right out of the gate. Hook them. Give them a reason to keep reading. You don't want to bleed readers in the first few pages.
2. Use good English. This isn't the streets, so don't "talk" that way. You can have characters that talk any way you please, of course. But outside the quotes, make your English teacher proud.
3. When your characters are talking, use quotes. When they are thinking, use italics. Don't confuse people. Sally said, "Let's go to Cabela's and stock up." Ben thought, *Woohoo! I found a great woman!* Just like that.
4. Notice how I wrote "Sally said" and "Ben thought." I didn't write "Sally yelled" or "Ben screamed." People are used to "said." So much so that they don't notice it, so it doesn't interrupt their reading process. Throw in changeups, and it will. Instead, you can write: Sally's nostrils flared, and her eyes squinted. She said, "Get over here now!" Now we know she's angry, and I didn't have to tell everyone. "Sally said angrily" is just bad.
5. Even though it's not real, you need to check your facts. You can't make things up about real objects, like cars. If you say a 1978 Jeep has a rolldown window in the back, a real 1978 Jeep better have a rolldown window in the back. Otherwise, you'll get lit up in the reviews. Check everything, no matter how small.

I've put down a lot of books because the author either bored me to tears or their writing was horrible. One time, I was done in a few paragraphs. Sometimes it takes a full chapter. I read books in KDP Select, so I'm not paying for the individual books.

The authors are getting paid by the pages I read. It's very important not to chase readers away. As Julie Broad says, #NoBoringBooks.

If you can't find a way to start with a bang, go back to the future. What? How many books have you seen this in: A book opens with an action scene, then you read the next heading, "Two months earlier" and you learn what led up to said action. It works well to capture readers.

As I said when I opened this section, if you've got an imagination, you can write fiction. Start small, and see what happens!

Writing Nonfiction

Success comes down to eliminating one word... three little letters... from your vocabulary.

Try.

You aren't TRYING to write a book. You are writing a book.

You aren't TRYING to build your business. You are building your business.

Make your word your bond. Commit to it. Now.

Julie Broad youtube.com/booklaunchers

Nonfiction is a whole different ballgame and even those without an imagination can do it. Guess what? You can do short reads for nonfiction too! I have a series of nonfiction books that are 5-10 pages each. Be clear in the description that it is a short book, however. I make it clear in the subtitle and description.

Nonfiction does require research, however. Fact checking fiction is a breeze compared to nonfiction. Fiction readers are looking to relax, for an escape from the real world. Nonfiction readers are looking for help with something. Giving them false, or bad information isn't helping them and doesn't look good for you.

It's easy to fix with a little research. Start off with a subject you know and would like to tell people about. Knowing the subject does not get you out of research and fact checking, however. You want to put out a good product, a great product. When you do, people will leave good reviews. If you put out garbage with misinformation, the reviews will not be kind to you.

I have seen some nasty reviews while doing research for books. Bad reviews don't only help the author of the book, but you and me too. I look for books in my niche with good review averages and books with bad averages. I read the good reviews to see what the author did right, then I read the bad ones to see what went wrong. I want to make sure I cover the good points in my book.

Also, I look for what was *missing* from the book. Reviewers will tell you what they wanted to read about. "I wish this book covered more about..." or "This book didn't talk about... at all." Those are the comments you're looking for; they are gold. Write those down. Then make sure you write about the topics. Mention in your description you cover those topics.

You can use a regular search engine to do your research but stay away from Wikipedia. It's fun for general knowledge, but it's not accurate enough for research. A better way to research, however, is scholar.google.com. That is where you'll find completed research on just about any subject.

It isn't Billy Bob's website with unverified information about UFOs. It's not Jane's opinion on the mating habits of the Mexican Staring Frog of Southern Sri Lanka. It's real research done by real researchers. You probably won't find anything about the carrying capacity of a legal rifle magazine in Nevada, but you might. I haven't looked. Probably not though. This is scientific research. For a lot of subjects, it's a blessing.

If you don't know what to write about, do your keyword

research. Look for keywords that don't have much competition but have people looking for them. Use your suggestion expander to see what people are looking for, remember. Or you can use Publisher Rocket, if you want your results fast - kevinbarry-maguire.com/Publisher-Rocket

Once you find your keyword, search the results on Amazon. Read the descriptions and reviews. Get ideas, never copy. Remember to find the good and bad in the reviews and act accordingly. Then hit up Google Scholar and see what you can find there. Then do a regular search on your favorite search engine. Hit up your local library and look at books and magazines there.

When you've gathered all your information, start writing. Writing is the easy part. If you're unsure of anything, fact check it. Don't guess. Guessing leads to bad reviews and worse - the Report button. Readers aren't paying you to guess. They can guess just as well as you can. They want accurate, reliable information.

You can write on just about anything if you do enough research. It won't make you an expert in a subject, so don't claim to be one. You should stay away from giving medical or legal advice. And never claim you're a doctor or lawyer, unless you are. Using a pen name does not give you the right to a medical or law degree. It can get you sued, however. You don't want that. I don't want that. Be cool.

Nonfiction books do not have to be as long as novels. Back when I started, the average was 12,000 words – or shorter than this chapter. Then it went up to around 20-25000 words because readers were complaining about book length. People were charging $19.99 for a 12,000-word paperback. Mine that size are $14.99 to $16.99, and I don't get any complaints.

Today, the average word count is 30,000 for nonfiction. Why? Because audiobooks happened, and they're on the rise. More and more people are listening to audiobooks. So why 30k words?

Audible.com is owned by Amazon and is the biggest audiobook seller out there. They pay authors by length of the audiobook. The best bang for the buck is a three-hour audiobook. The royalty almost doubles from the next step down.

The average narrator reads at 9700 words per hour. That means you need a book of at least 29,100 words to hit the magic three hours. So people are rounding up to 30k. They aren't leaving room for error though. The average narrator reads at an average pace. Some read faster and those 30k words won't be enough to hit three hours. Don't be one of those. I know how fast I narrate and 30k is enough for me. A book of 32-33k words is a lot safer. But we'll get into that in the audiobook chapter.

Another bonus of writing 30k word books is you *can* charge $19.99 (or more) for your paperback book.

Pricing

That's a great lead-in to talk about pricing. You can start your fiction and nonfiction eBooks at $2.99 for the most part. My very short, short reads are 99 cents, and I doubt that will ever change. I have fiction short reads at $2.99; those are 16k words and more. I returned Book 1 to 99 cents about six months ago.

If those books start selling well, you can raise the fiction to $3.99 and leave it there. I have seen some at $4.99, but they're established. I have a nonfiction eBook at $5.99, and it sells regularly. I could probably raise it another dollar, but I'm ok with it where it is. I have others I raised to $4.99, and they do well. I always raise by $1 and wait. If sales slowdown a lot, I'd lower it back to the previous level. That hasn't happened yet though.

My plan for this book is to have it at 99 cents for pre-order, and it will open up at $3.99, and I plan to increase it up to $5.99. The paperback, I'll try to time availability the same time as the eBook. Paperback doesn't get a pre-order so I can't pick the day it goes live. That's all in Amazon's hands. I'll upload it two days before the eBook goes live and pray.

The price will open at $16.99 and will gradually increase to $19.99. If it sells well enough at that price, I will increase it again. This is how you should be pricing all your books. Start low to attract buyers and gain traction and raise your BSR. Then increase gradually. FYI, the royalty 2at $19.99 is about $10, depending on page count.

Most people use 6x9 for nonfiction books. If your page count is hurting your profit, however, you can jump to 8x10 or even 8.5x11. I think this book will be 8x10. It's hard to tell because I write in 8.5x11 and a size 16 font. I like to lean back in my chair as I write, it helps my shoulder. But I also need to see what I'm writing. The paperback will have an 11 or 12 font. eBook readers choose their own font size.

We put a lot of time into these books; we want to get paid for our efforts, right? A high page count is a good thing. It gives the readers an idea of how big the book is. They will rarely look at the trim size and may not even consider that size matters. But page count eats at your profits too. It's a delicate dance of trim size, font choice, and font size.

Some fonts are bigger than others and will take up more pages. You can't use too small of a font size, or people will have trouble reading. Too big, and they'll complain that you're trying to pad the pages. If they only knew we're trying to keep the pages down! At age 42, I started needing reading glasses. That is another reason I like to keep the font around 12. I'm certainly not alone in needing glasses to read, so a bigger font can let us take them off if we keep a modest distance from the book.

Book reviews are one of the greatest ways to gain social proof and assist potential buyers in purchasing your book. Should it be the primary focus for your book business? No. But, review gathering should be at least a small yet consistent part of your author business plan.

Dale L Roberts

kevinbarrymaguire.com/Dales-Startup

Ghostwriters

Ways to 10X Your Non-Fiction Book Investment.

Of course, it depends on your goals and your business, but realistically the right book positioned well can easily lead to:

- *10 paid speaking gigs,*
- *20 new clients,*
- *Charging higher prices for what you do,*
- *a strategic partnership that expands your business dramatically,*
- *media exposure which attracts new customers to your business,*
- *capital for your business (if you're a real estate investor this could be a game changer!), or*
- *brand extensions, like swag, courses, or workshops*

could all be easy ways to get a big return.

The person who is known as 'the person' to hire for something can charge far more for the exact same service than someone who isn't known.

Julie Broad booklaunchers.com

What are ghost writers? They aren't in the sky. Sorry, that's another old song reference. A much better one than the previous song. If you don't want to write books but want to be able to sell them on Amazon, (and elsewhere) you can hire a ghostwriter. That person will write the book, and you get to take the credit and keep all the royalties.

What's in it for the author? He or she gets paid in a lump sum before you get to publish it. Remember when I said there are authors and publishers? If you are hiring ghost writers, you're a publisher. If you've successfully published some books and are making a decent income, you can expand your business by hiring a ghostwriter.

Say you've got a fiction or nonfiction series going and doing well. You want another series, but you don't have the time to get it done? Ghostwriter. Lots of authors you know use ghostwriters. It's normal. I've used them for some nonfiction because writing fiction is more fun. But nonfiction can bring in the dollars too. I want some of that pie.

Most authors will put their name on books written by ghostwriters. I feel weird doing that. If my name is on it, I wrote it. But just because I use a pen name doesn't mean I didn't write it. I've written most of my books, even the meditation books. Only one of those is on my website.

Some people go to Upwork to hire ghostwriters. I've heard mostly good about them, but I've heard a few horror stories too. Only a few. I have never used Upwork so I can't give any first-hand knowledge there. It can be cheaper than using a company, but it comes with more risk.

There are several ghostwriting companies, and I've used three of them. My favorite, by far, is The Urban Writers. They have a new service called, "The Marketplace" where they sell books already written, no waiting for the author to research and write.

Those books are edited and proofread, checked for plagiarism, and come with suggested titles and descriptions. Even though it's already edited, check it. Always. It's your reputation and reviews on the line. All writing companies check for plagiarism. It's one of the pluses for using a company vs. Upwork or other freelance sites.

Editing usually costs more and is not included with a freelancer. All of The Urban Writers packages come with proofreading and editing. Although, the cheapest package (new writers) says "light proofreading and editing." It's still better than the others, who don't offer editing at all.

I order the Urban Package and have no issues with the writing. The more expensive packages have more experienced writers. Go with what you feel comfortable with.

You will have to prepare a solid outline for the writer to follow. Well, you don't have to, but you really should. I strongly encourage it. Do your keyword research the same as if you were going to write it. Check the competition's titles, descriptions, and reviews. I also write the description and instruct the writer to make sure the book agrees with the description.

Now write your outline. Show how you'd like the book to look, chapter titles help. Give them everything they need to make your book the way you want it, because there are no re-writes. The writer will write what you tell them, so tell them. Don't be shy. Most of them don't bite.

One thing I do is change the titles when I get the book in my possession. I'll give a sample title when making my order, but never the real title. It's a "just in case" maneuver. I don't want the writer to be able to find it on Amazon, just in case he or she becomes a disgruntled ex-employee.

Getting Reviews the Right Way

Getting good reviews can be tough. It can be a long, slow crawl, especially with no and low-content books. We've already discussed the wrong way – paying for them. You've worked hard on your books and your account, don't lose it over reviews.

The first way is to ask in all your books. It can be hard in no-content as there really isn't anywhere to ask. At the end of the book, thank the reader for purchasing and reading your book. Say some nice things and tell them reviews help authors, because they do. I've shown you how, so we're good there. Ask them to write an *honest review*. That's it. Do not ask for a positive review, a five-star review, or any other kind of review. You are only allowed to ask for an honest review.

Do not offer gifts of any kind for a review. Amazon doesn't allow that either. Don't ask your friends and family for reviews, Amazon knows who they are in most cases and will remove the reviews. Fun fact: Amazon owns Goodreads. If you sign into Goodreads with Facebook, Amazon knows all your friends and family.

Another way Amazon knows your friends and family is if you copy the link to your book and paste it in emails, Facebook, Twitter, etc. You have to "clean" the link first, because people you don't know could also use that link and leave a review. Then Amazon will delete it, thinking you know the person.

I checked out the top selling book for this example link. Today, that book is *Where the Crawdads Sing*, by Delia Owens. She has almost 40,000 reviews with a five-star average. That's amazing. This is what it looks like when you copy and paste: https://www.amazon.com/dp/B078GD3DRG/ref=chrt_bk_s-d_fc_1_ci_lp

That ref tells Amazon a lot. That's what you need to clean to make a good, sharable link: https://www.amazon.com/dp/B078GD3DRG

Both those links will take you to the same book, but one won't tell Amazon you searched it… the clean one, of course. That is the link you'll show to your readers so the reviews will stick.

If you're building an email list, you can ask for ARC readers for your next book. ARC is Advanced Review Copy. You give readers a free PDF of your book, and they agree to leave an honest review for you. There's that word again. Use it. Every time. You also tell your ARC team to mention that they "received a free copy of the book in exchange for an honest review." Amazon allows this but only for books. Don't try it with anything else Amazon does.

You can give free copies of your book to anyone in exchange for an honest review. Don't limit yourself to email. If you're in relevant Facebook groups, offer it there. But have people message you for the pdf, don't just post it for anyone to download.

Netgalley.com is another place to get honest reviews, but it'll cost ya. It's an expensive service, but the reviews are real. They come from real readers who sign up to read books for free and leave reviews.

Finally, your email list that I know you're building. Yeah, that's another topic for later. Just assume you're building it. You can ask your list to review your books. When they sign up for the list, you send them a welcome email. In that email, give a subtle reminder for a review. If you choose a service with an autoresponder, then you can set an email to fire off a few weeks later, asking again. Always ask for an honest review.

Chapter 4 Exercises, Part II

Yep, I told you there would be a part II, and here it is! But this is cool; you'll like this one because I'm giving you a choice. I'm nice like that. Because the chapter is so long and covers a lot of different topics, you get the choose what you're going to do.

You can choose low-content, fiction, or nonfiction. Do the keyword research and find a title, subtitle, and your seven keywords. Make it good, because later you'll be writing them, or making the interior. Or even hiring a ghostwriter. You can make them short reads too, if you like. It is a great way to break yourself in.

So now that we're at the end of the chapter, are you curious to see what the final word count for Chapter 4 is? I sure am. I think when I mentioned it earlier, it was at 8000 words. Well, the final tally is 15,600. Wow, that's longer than a lot of nonfiction books out there... all in one chapter!

KDP Courses:

Dale L Roberts DIY Course: kevinbarrymaguire.com/Dales-Startup

The Publishing Evolution: kevinbarrymaguire.com/Publishing-Evolution

CHAPTER 5 MERCH

*M*erch by Amazon is not a "get rich quick" option by any means. It's a slow roll. So why do it? Because with a little patience and nurturing, it can make you a lot of money. When you're first accepted to Merch, you're in Tier 10, meaning you're allowed a whopping ten shirt designs live on Amazon. There is a limit of 1 design upload per day in Tier 10. That may have changed in the last change. It did in Tier 500. In order to get to Tier 25, you must sell ten t-shirts.

Tier 10 is the hardest one to get out of. First, it takes you ten days to upload all your allowable designs. Then your ten designs need to be seen in a sea of millions of t-shirts available on Amazon. It's rough. But it's doable, especially if you do it differently than I did!

What? Yeah, I took some bad advice and didn't realize it until a few months ago. I was told to keep my prices low, and I'd sell more shirts. It's sounds great, in theory. In practice, Amazon shoppers aren't bottom feeders. They'll pay more for higher quality – even though the quality is all the same. They think *higher price, better quality*. That's how they make their purchases.

I was selling all my shirts for $14.99 and making a tiny profit, trading "faster" tier ups for royalties. Today, my shirts start at $16.99, Amazon's default price on our dashboards. My most expensive shirt is $19.99, and that's a nice royalty when it hits!

Another mistake I was making involved the way I did my bullet points. I was told by the same two guys (twins) how to do my bullet points, and it was killing my sales. Again, that was a few months ago when I figured it out. I had help figuring that out. I started listening to someone else, who I'll talk about later. Everything in your bullet points is searchable. They're essentially keyword slots.

So, it took me about a year to reach Tier 500, and I've been on that tier for almost a year, a real slow grind that didn't have to be. Don't make my mistakes, and it will go much faster for you. I know people who started the same time as me and are Tier 2000 and Tier 4000. You'll meet one of them later too.

In the past few months, I've doubled my total sales. In two or three months, I should have the 500 total sales I need to jump into Tier 1000. That will be exciting! I earn between $65 and $100 a month now, so potentially doubling that income will be nice. I still consider Merch my "coffee" money, but I know it will be much more in time.

Another reason I started selling more shirts is because I left Photoshop and started using a vector program, Affinity Designer. Designer allows me to put out higher quality designs because vectors don't pixelate.

Designer and Adobe Illustrator are paid vector software. They're made for drawing, not photographs. On the free side, you can check out Ink Scape, Gravit, and Vectr. Vectr is an online software, no download necessary. I have only used Designer and can't tell you anything about the others, unfortunately.

· · ·

Your First Design

Way back at the start of this book, I asked you to sign up for Merch at merch.amazon.com. Hopefully, you've done so and maybe even have been accepted already. Either way, now is a good time to create your first design.

Keyword research is the same as books, except now you're looking at shirts. You already have the AMZ Suggestion Expander; make use of it. Just about anything you can think of is a niche, and you can use your no and low-content niches for Merch. In Merch, the BSR's should be between 100,000 and 700,000. If you find lower without much competition, you're in for good times.

Merch designs are 4500x5400 pixels (15" x 18") and 300 dpi. Amazon wants rgb instead of cmyk. Finally, your .png must be less than 25mb. That's easy, I've never gone over, and at Tier 500, I've made at least 600 designs. Probably more. All your designs will be uploaded to Amazon as .png files.

Ok, fire up your chosen software and open a new document with the dimensions above and 300 dpi. If you can't change to a transparent background later, start with a transparent back-ground. All your designs must have a transparent background when uploaded.

We're going to make a birthday design because they're ever-green – meaning they sell all year round. Lots of people are having birthdays every single day. Once again, I'll be going off the top of my head. I do have birthday shirts of my own, of course. I won't be using those. Once again, I must guard my keywords – you should too!

I came up with Thirty and Flirty for a shirt design. I did check for trademarks, and it's clear. So, you can upload this if you choose. You'll still have to make sure your bullet points are trademark free. You'll also need to change the design somewhat, make it unique. Everyone reading this can't upload the exact same design.

This design will be all text for several reasons. One, they're easy and great for breaking in new t-shirt designers. Two, they sell. Simple sells. Over half of my 500 designs are text only. If you do use images, don't go overboard. One is fine in most cases. But make it big. Don't make people squint to see it.

Click the text icon in your software, usually a T, and type in "Thirty" anywhere. Then make a new line and type either "&" or "and." I prefer "&" for this. Make one more line and type "Flirty." Capitalize like a title, either every word starting with a cap or all the words except and, or, and the.

You should have three text layers in your layers panel - usually on the right side of your screen. For something short like this, I like having every word on its own layer. That way I can move them around as I see fit. It also makes changing colors easier if you choose to make a word stand out with a different color, which you may want to do. I just read an article saying bright colors are in for 2020.

For this design, I would move "Thirty" to the top and just off center, to the left. Then I would move "Flirty" below, maybe a ¼ inch and off center to the right. For the ampersand (&) I'd find a spot below "Thirty, and to the left. Move it around and see how it looks in different places. This is why it's good for it to have its own layer.

Now that you have the look how you want it, it's time to mess with the font. Flirty brings up romance in my mind, and romance means a pretty script for a font. Cursive and flowing. Finding a script font good for shirts is hard but not impossible. Thin lines are out. They'll be hard to read and fade fast, leaving unhappy customers. Those are the ones who leave bad reviews.

I use Font Cloud from Creative Fabrica to look at my fonts and choose the right one - kevinbarrymaguire.com/creative-fabrica. When you're on their website, click "Tools" at the top of the screen, then "Font Cloud" from the dropdown. It's free, so no worries there. I have it bookmarked because I use it for every design, shirt, and low content covers I make. You do have to load your own fonts.

The first one I came across that I like is "Christmas Wish Calligraphy." "Hariston" has possibilities. It looks like the Dirty Dancing font. "Swindon" is the last of the fonts I have that would do good on this shirt. I'm going to go with Christmas Wish but Hariston is also a good choice. If I were uploading this, I might make a shirt with both fonts. Don't do that starting out; you have too few slots.

Highlight the first word and change the font to something you have and like. Then do it for the other two. The ampersand may look better in a different font, that's something you're going to have to look at. You'll also have to reset your word placement as the font change will affect the size of your words.

Now it's time to play with the color. Remember, you'll be designing for a black t-shirt, so white always looks good and is the base color for most shirts. I have found that after white, teal and light blue sell the best for me. But it's 2020 now and maybe the article is right. Maybe bright colors will do the trick now. Play around with the colors and see what works. A lot of the time, I'll only change one or two words, and they'll balance each other if it's two words.

I took a few minutes and made the design too. My finished product is different than what I typed, and that's ok. A lot of times, you'll have an idea and by the time you're done, you've changed your mind 100 times. I've had several shirts where I bought illustrations from Deposit Photos only to have the final design nothing but text - kevinbarrymaguire.com/deposit-photos.

As you'll see in figure 5-1, I kept the font white. Remember, simple sells. But I added a swash under "Flirty" and made that a deep red, hinting at lipstick. You could experiment with a set of red lips there too. I also put it behind Flirty but dragged the layer below the word. In Designer, you'll have to be careful not to drag it into the layer you're moving under. You'll know it when it happens; whatever you moved will disappear. It will be nested into the other layer. You'll learn when to do that if you take a course on Designer.

The final thing I did was change the ampersand to "and." I tried moving the ampersand everywhere. I changed the size a few times. Nothing worked; it looked out of place.

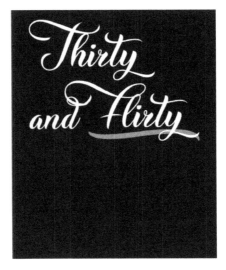

Figure 5-1

I also like how the tails of the "d" on "and" and the "F" on Flirty" mix with each other. On this design I would keep all the words the same color. Changing one would set it off balance. On a final note, I got the swash from a font called "Mostley." Some fonts you download from Creative Fabrica will come with a lot of variations, italic, bold, etc. Some of those extras include swash fonts, sometimes called, "extras." For my swash, the font is called, "Mostley Swash." Every character on the keyboard gives a different look. The one I used is my favorite; it's the "u" key. Small "u."

On a final note for this design, remember your final product will be a transparent .png file. I showed black so you can see it −

and black is the most purchased color on Amazon. I always check to make sure the design will look good on navy, blue, pink, and purple too. I won't be uploading this as a t-shirt to help keep the competition down, should you want to. I may upload it as a PopSocket, however. A quick word on PopSocket: never use that name in your listings. Amazon doesn't allow it because it's trademarked. You can use "phone grip" if you like. I do, though I'm not sure it helps. Amazon adds "PopSocket" to the title for you anyway, so no worries. I don't think you start out with PopSockets though. They were released while I was in Tier 25, and I got them in Tier 50.

Step It Up

Ok, what will you do when you get out of Tier 25 and now have 50 slots to fill? I remember struggling to come up with ideas back then, but I was mostly driving blind. I wasn't following anyone for Merch yet and didn't know what I was doing half the time.

One thing I started doing was looking at people's t-shirts as I was walking around in stores, or anywhere else. Every shirt you see is a bona fide idea. Someone liked the design enough to pay money for that shirt. The catch, of course, is most shirt designs are copyright or trademark protected. Sports teams, movies, comics, Disney, etc. are all things you need to stay away from. There are more of course, but I can't list them all here. If you're unsure, always check before uploading.

Amazon keeps track of how many rejections you get and what type. If you get too many, especially early on, it's good-bye time. I don't want to scare you away, but I do want you to know the threat is real. Play it safe, and you'll be ok.

I saw a guy in a Facebook group ask why his journals were being blocked. Amazon only blocks for trademark violations, that I know of. It's serious infractions. I asked him what he was uploading, and he said, "Movie titles and music bands." Oy. I'm shocked he still has an account. I told him that, and that he's probably on the last of his nine lives. You can't do that on KDP or Merch.

Are you on Facebook? Pay attention to the memes, current events, and advertised t-shirts. These are great, and I've sold shirts by taking ideas from Facebook. Don't copy the meme exactly, but make something about the meme. As for the advertised t-shirts, check for trademarks before making any designs. I don't know how many times I've done the reverse and wasted my time on designs. Check, then make.

Current events are good for quick sales. I got in early on the "OK Boomer" thing because I paid attention to what was being said. I made about five easy text designs and uploaded them. Three of the five got sales and one did really well.

I tried to get in early on Jeffrey Epstein but got that rejection. That still irks me. Others made a lot of money on that, but I was not allowed to join the fun. I did ok with the "Storm Area 51" thing, but it faded fast.

Political shirts do ok but don't limit yourself to your party of choice. You can, of course, but you're leaving money on the table. Use different brand names for each party. The brand names are like pen names on KDP. Nobody will be able to track them to you, so feel free to do as you wish.

Another way to step up your game is to pay someone else to do the research. I use Merch Money Masters for this - kevinbarrymaguire.com/Merch-Money. It saves me a lot of time, and I get a lot of proven ideas, with links to the shirts. If you use my link, you'll get $5 off your purchase. When you go back, use the code KEVIN for the $5 off.

All the links are checked for trademark already, so you're good there. They also list any keywords they find. Once again, use the links for inspiration; do not copy – make them better.

One of the mistakes I made when using the Merch Money

research was ignoring designs I didn't like. It took me a while to realize it's not about me. People are buying these designs whether I like them or not. When I learned that, I started making more sales.

You can search YouTube for Merch ideas. One of the experts you've seen, Ryan A Raymond, has a great YouTube channel for Merch, and he's breaking into Ignite too. That's a bonus.

Back to Facebook. You have friends, I assume. Most of us do, even Eric Cartman has Facebook friends. You need ideas and sales. The need to tier up is an insatiable beast. Ask your friends and family what t-shirts they'd like to see. Ask for requests. Create them, then post them and tag the person making the request. Some won't buy them, but some will.

When you have designs that have been up for at least three months with no sales, it may be time to recycle them. Create a new design for each non-seller. Delete the ones in question, and immediately upload the new designs. Besides the obvious, getting fresh designs up, it tells Amazon you're still there.

Amazon likes busy accounts, and it's said they will show your stuff more. I do see an uptick in sales after I do this. Some people say all you need to do is change a few prices, and that's probably true. I trust one of the people saying it – Kelli Roberts. The thing is, I rarely change prices unless a design has sold a lot. Then, just as with books, I'll raise the price by $1. I've brought a few shirts up to $18.99 that way. They still sell well, but not enough for me to raise the price again. I may have found the right price for them.

When I started, Amazon would delete your designs if they didn't sell after 90 days. Then they moved it to six months, and now it's a year. I like that; it gives designs time to prove themselves. But I will still knock out designs when I need room for fresh ones and when my sales slow up. I like to remind Amazon I'm still in the game. I have had a design sell the day Amazon was going to delete it. It hasn't sold since. It was funny though. I was going to delete it the day before but saw one that was going to fall off that day. It got the ax instead, and I got another step closer to Tier 1000!

Should you delete designs that have already sold? I don't. I have two designs that sold when I was in Tier 10 and not a single sale since. They're still there. You not only need the number of sales in your tier to tier up, you need to have your slots full or mostly full. Right now, I have 500 slots full (always) and am waiting to make 500 sales. This month, February, has been brutal. So all those shirts and PopSockets that have sold, stay. I have over 100 permanent slots filled. I like that.

How do I know what has sold and what hasn't? I remember most of them, but I have Pretty Merch Pro to tell me the rest - kevinbarrymaguire.com/Pretty-Merch. It shows me what has sold and what hasn't. It also tells me when designs are about to drop off – when Amazon deletes them. You need to expand the filters on the Products tab to see that. Right now, I'm good for at least three months.

That is the tab I use to find my next deletions. You can't delete from that screen, however. I copy the title and go to the "Manage" tab, then paste it in the search there. Then I find what I need and delete it. That way I never accidently delete a design that has sold. I thought I did once and freaked out.

I was using an extension that you could delete from its "manage" page. But when I did so, it showed a different product as being the deleted one. I stopped using it immediately. I've also heard this one can get our accounts deleted, so it's good I stopped using it. I stick to approved extensions now.

Final Tips

Remember, getting out of Tier 10 fast is your goal. Buy your own shirts if you must. If you know you're going to do this in advance, set the price as low as you can. Buy them, then raise the prices.

Always check for trademarks. Check your title and everything in your bullet points. (I'm drilling this into your heads.)

Check Pinterest and Etsy for t-shirt ideas.

Keep up on new trends.

Learn your design software – YouTube and Udemy are good for this - kevinbarrymaguire.com/Udemy.

Be patient. This is the slowest platform to grow, but it is worth it. This will slowly grow to thousands of dollars a month. You'll be hiring help in the higher tiers!

It was a strange day when I realized I'm an employer. Not for merch so much (yet), but I have hired a few freelancers on Workana for specific designs. I do hire people on the other platforms. Always hire freelancers though. That way, you aren't responsible for their taxes.

Finally, check out this help page on Amazon - bit.ly/Merch-Help. It shows you a lot of helpful tips on font usage and some do's and don'ts.

Chapter 5 Exercise

This exercise is designed for you to be ready when you're accepted into Merch. Research and design ten designs. Don't make them all one niche. For the first ten, you should have ten different niches. Put them up and see which ones work for you and adjust from there. If you take a design down, save it for when you have more slots available. This is fun work, so have fun!

Ryan A Raymond has a YouTube channel full of great videos about Merch, and a few on Ignite. In this video, Ryan shows you five ways to promote your shirts, https://bit.ly/Ryan-Shirt

CHAPTER 6 ACX

There are more audiobook companies besides ACX. ACX is owned by Amazon, and they get our audiobooks onto Amazon, Audible.com, and iTunes. We'll talk about those other options in chapter 9, Going Wide. ACX is the easiest audiobook platform to get started on, so here we are!

Special note: ACX limits countries to the United States, Canada, UK, and Ireland. But no worries, in the Going Wide chapter, I'll show you where you can participate in audiobooks.

There have been some people (the twins) who taught people outside those countries to go around the rules. Don't listen to them. There is a reason ACX doesn't want to hear their names and banned them. They will still catch you and freeze your account. Follow the rules and avoid heartache and headache.

Narrator

There are two ways to make money on ACX, and the first one I'll discuss is being a narrator. That's when you record someone else's audiobook (or even your own.) I do both.

Stop. I know what you're saying, "I hate my voice!" Yeah, we all do. That doesn't stop people from doing it though, does it? If that were the case, nobody would be doing voiceovers. You get used to it once you've listened to yourself 100 times while editing.

You don't have a $1000 microphone? Neither do I. I use a Blue Yeti and have never had a file rejected. I would use the Yeti as a starting point, don't go lower. I used a Blue Snowball once, bad idea. I also strongly recommend using a pop filter. They aren't expensive, but you can make them yourself if you prefer. Check YouTube for DIY pop filter.

The only software I use is Audacity. It's free and has a lot of useful plugins available. The plugins I use and can't do without are Compress Dynamics, De-Clicker, Limiter, RMS Normalize, and ACX Check. You will need each one of those. Installation is easy, just follow the instructions here - bit.ly/insall-plugin.

If you don't have a sound-proof room or can't afford a sound booth, no worries. I use a cardboard box with sound foam glued to the inside. I have a small hole in the back to put my mic cord through. It doesn't knock out all sound, but it does a good enough job. If a dog barks, you're going to have to repeat the line. Again, YouTube is your friend; do a simple search for DIY sound box.

Caution Marquiza (the cat) has made it her life's mission to destroy that box. She does not like the foam. If you have a cat, make sure to store the box where cats can't get to it.

So now you've got Audacity and all those plugins installed, a microphone, and some sound dampening. You're ready to make a recording. Fire up Audacity and get comfortable. Sit up straight so your lungs and throat aren't crunched. You want free flow of air for a clean, clear voice.

Find something to read and make a recording. Speak for a few minutes so you make a few mistakes and have something to edit. Here's the key to making fewer mistakes: Go slow. That's it.

Going slow has benefits for you, your client, and the listener.

It's a win-win-win. When you think you're reading slow enough, you probably aren't. It took me a while to figure out just how slow was slow enough. I'd listen to myself, and it sounded like I was racing through the lines. But I "knew" I had read slow.

We know the benefits of reading slow for you, fewer mistakes. What about your client (or you again if it's your book) and the listener? First, the listener. When you're listening to someone read, do you prefer the newscaster who's trying to read 60 seconds of words in 30 seconds? Or the soft, easy voice of someone relaxed? Most people want to hear the relaxed voice, especially when listening to an audiobook. It's too easy to miss the details with fast talkers.

Now onto the client, the person's book you're narrating. If you haven't noticed, a lot of nonfiction books today are the same length, about 30,000 words. That was the goal of this book too, but I've already passed that mark. What is the deal with 30,000 words? The deal is, it's a three-hour audiobook.

Most people read at 9700 words per hour. I was much faster and had to train myself to go slower, as mentioned above. So a three-hour audiobook would be 29,100 words. Those 30,000 don't leave much room for error, and authors will let you know to hit three-hours. Two-hours and fifty-nine minutes won't cut it. It must be three.

Here's why: ACX pays rights-holders by the length of an audiobook. If your audiobook is under an hour, the pay is dismal. From one-hour to two-hours and 59 minutes, it gets a little better, but still meh. But the pay about doubles when you have an audiobook that is three-hours to four-hours and 59 minutes. Cha-ching. The same thing does not happen when you cross five-hours. It is better to write two 30,000-word books than to write a five-hour book. The next jump isn't until ten hours.

So, you make fewer mistakes, the author – or rights holder – makes more money, and the listener has a better listening experience. Read slow.

. . .

Editing

You've got your recording, and you're ready to edit. There are three ways to edit that I know of, and I've tried them all. The first one I tried involved a clicker, and I did that for a long time. Jason will show you (in the video) how it's done - bit.ly/Edit-Audio-ACX. He'll also show you how to set up Compress Dynamics. And he'll show you how to set up a macro for using Normalize and Compress Dynamics. He does it at the end, but I do it at the start because it shows me all the pops and clicks. All that said, I don't use the clicker anymore. It's too slow.

There is another way that says to stop on every mistake, then make a new track to continue. Whew. Talk about slow. I read through most mistakes now. It only makes sense because you must listen to the whole track anyway. So I listen and edit at the same time. If I make a mistake, I stop for a second then read the line again and move on.

If I've made the same mistake three times, I'll stop the recording. There is either a mistake in the writing or my head can't wrap around what is being said. It's usually the writing. I have seen some really bad writing while recording audiobooks. I weed out the worst ones during the audition. If I see too many errors, I stop that audition. I'm not reading a full book of bad English. It would take too long and drop my pay per hour.

I delete the mistakes I just made to speed up the editing process. When I think I have the line right, I start recording and move on. One chapter at a time. Speaking of bad writing, you're going to need to decide: Will you edit bad English or not? Most narrators will not; they will read through all mistakes. I will correct obvious errors while I read, but that's it. You should do the same. We aren't getting paid to edit their work, only to narrate it. Editing takes time and will reduce your pay. It's up to the rights holders to give you a book that is ready to go.

The first thing I do is check the entire recording for the lines Audacity adds when you stop, then start recording again. I wish they didn't do that. You need to get rid of them, clicking on them will do it. If you don't, everything I'm about to tell you to do, you'll have to do again. The effects only work between any of those lines that are still showing. We get rid of them, so we only do it once. But before we do that, we need to do one more thing. Get rid of all the large, empty spaces. Delete those long breaks, any throat clearings, and obvious pops. Those won't be obvious to you for a while, however. Pops can look like a t, d, or k at the end of a word. Those sounds have a small space between themselves and the main word. You don't want to accidently get rid of them. Leave some space at the beginning or end of the file. It will come in handy in a few minutes.

Ok, now that the preparation is out of the way, we can get into the editing. Double click in the wave area to select the whole file. Now go to Effect > Compress Dynamics on the dropdown – it will be near the bottom. On short files, it should go quick. After about eight minutes, everything gets slower.

Next, Effect > Normalize. It will be in the top of the Effect section, in alphabetical order. The whole file should still be selected. When that is done, find a few inches of space without audio waves. Because you listened and left space at the start or finish, that would be a great spot to use. Highlight that space and go to File > Noise Reduction. On the popup, click "Get Noise Profile" at the top. Now you have to repeat the Effect > Noise Reduction. Only this time, click "Ok." You should see the noise disappear. Or most of it.

Click in the middle of the empty space and then the Play button. Don't do it from the start of a file or from inside audio waves. If you can hear any noise, repeat the Noise Reduction process. Get the new profile, then go back to the popup, and click "Ok." Twice usually does it for me.

Next, you'll go back to Effect and go to the bottom for De-

Clicker. I use the default settings except for Sensitivity Threshold. I change that to three. Any higher, and it will miss a lot of the clicks and pops inside the waves. Those are hard to remove manually, and most times, I have to re-record the phrase. Any lower and you could write a book while it's removing the clicks. Yep, this one takes time, even on short files. Walk away and make some coffee, play with the kids, walk your dog, watch paint dry. Anything but stare at the slow-moving progress. But it's worth the wait. This plugin is awesome.

Now go to the beginning of the file and click Play. The Spacebar is also a play/pause hotkey. It's faster to use the Space-bar, especially when you'll be using CTRL a lot. I have my right hand on the mouse and left hand ready with CTRL. It's just a quick pinky shot to hit the Spacebar. What does CTRL do? I'm glad you asked. It's your friend. If you hear a pop that De-Clicker missed, highlight it and press CTRL to add silence over it. It's used when you can't delete the pop because the pause between words would be too short. Add silence over it instead.

You should either have headphones on or the volume up. Headphones are the better option. You're listening for whatever doesn't belong, those pops and clicks mostly, but also, any other noises the mic may have picked up. Any time you come across a noise that may appear more than once, do a Noise Reduction cycle over it. Then a CTRL if that didn't get rid of it completely. I should mention there is an Add Silence icon up on the menu bar. It looks like a barbell. I don't know where it will be on your copy, however. I have customized mine.

If you get a nasty pop inside a word, click CTRL to open a new window. Record the phrase again, then do your compress, normalize, and noise reduction over the new file. Then copy it and paste it over the bad one in the original file. It may sound louder than the rest of the file, so that needs to be fixed too.

As you're going through, delete your mistakes. With the clicker method, you're deleting mistakes, then listening to the file.

It takes too much time. When you get to the end, your editing should be done. Congrats!

Now we have to finish it up. Double click in the wave file to select all, then go to Effect > Limiter. It's at the bottom. When that's done and the entire file still selected, go to Analyze on the menu bar up top, then ACX Check. If all went well, it will say, "Clip meets ACX requirement." If not, there are a few more things you need to do. No worries, we'll get you there.

If it says something about the Peak level, run the limiter again. Then ACX Check to make sure it was enough. If not, do it again. Twice is all I've ever had to do it. If it says the RMS level is wrong, run Effect > RMS Normalize. You'll need to follow that with a Limiter or two. If it says the Noise Floor is too high, you need to find a clean spot and run Noise Reduction. It's picking up too much noise.

You're almost done. ACX likes the start and end of the files to have room tone. They require .5 seconds to 1 second at the start and 1-5 seconds at the end. I make it easy on myself and maintain consistency by using one second at the start and five seconds at the end.

I do it by deleting the front of the file, until I reach a wave. I'll have already selected one second of clean space and done a CTRL on the selection. Then copied it (CTRL.) I paste that one second of time at the start. Then, after the chapter name (also required), I delete all the space until the talking starts again. Then I paste three of those seconds in that space.

If you're keeping up, you now have one second of clean space at the start and three seconds after the chapter name. Now go to the end of the file and delete the empty space. Add your five seconds now. Now the file is ready to be uploaded.

Make sure everything passes the ACX Check. If one of your files is rejected, it is up to you to fix it. You and the author will get an email telling you which file(s) didn't pass. The author will probably send you a message too. Stop what you're doing and fix it. Their audiobook goes to the back of the line when a file doesn't pass.

The upload process is pretty simple. It's a walk in the park. Type in the chapter name (unless the author has already done it) then upload the file. It helps to name the files with numbers. So the opening credits are 01_Opening Credits every time for me. The introduction would be 02_Introduction, and so on. It keeps everything nice and neat when uploading. You aren't searching for what goes next.

ACX Standards

You can look up the ACX standards, and I suggest you do - bit.ly/ACX-Standards. But I'll give you the list:

- Be consistent in overall sound and formatting
- Be comprised of all mono or all stereo files
- Include opening and closing credits
- Include a retail sample that is between one and five minutes long
- Be recorded by a human

Each uploaded audio file must:

- Be a 192 kbps or higher MP3, constant bit rate (CBR) at 44.1 kHz
- Contain only one chapter/section that is shorter than 120 minutes
- Section header must be read aloud
- Have room tone at the head and at the tail
- Be free of extraneous sounds
- Measure between -23dB and -18dB RMS
- Have-3dB peak values
- Have a maximum -60dB noise floor

Most of these are straight-forward or are accomplished using Audacity with the plugins I've suggested. But I'll go over a few of them. For Audiobooks, choose Mono when recording. You probably don't have a stereo mic setup, so don't choose it. The files are smaller too, bonus.

Opening and closing credits are easy and only take a few seconds. ACX tells you exactly what to say on the file upload page (Produce Audiobook tab.) They're at the bottom of the page.

Retail audio samples are what potential customers listen to. Most people use the Introduction. Boooring. There are two better ways of handling this: 1. Choose the best part of the book and use it. 2. Use the book description. Only use the book description if it rocks.

I don't know who has two-hour chapters, but I did come close in Chapter four. I'm still splitting it up, however. Editing a 15k word audio file doesn't seem like too much fun to me. The effects would take minutes each. The de-clicker would take all night. I could write a book while it was doing its thing!

Section header is almost always the chapter title and/or number.

How Much Should You Charge?

Great question, and one that isn't easy to answer. I did my first one for $40 per finished hour (pfh). It was a one-hour audiobook, so I was paid $40. I won't do that again. I was still recording with the clicker, so it took me extra long to edit. It took about two hours to record and four or five to edit. Yikes. I made a little over $5 per hour on that one.

Per finished hour is how narrators are paid when paid up front. The length of the finished product is what is used. For a three-hour audiobook, you will get paid your rate x 3. It probably took you five hours or more to record, and six to edit. So, your hourly rate is much lower than your pfh rate.

You will need to pick up some jobs, so start as low as you dare, but I would never go below $40. You're worth more than that even as a newbie. You're worth more than $40 too, but you need to attract that first client. It's a great way to get sample audio files up for your profile. Your first one will have to be you reading a book you have rights to, or one in the public domain.

After you get a few under your belt, charge more. $50 pfh should be the lowest from then on. Then keep raising it as you go. The more you charge, the fewer hits you'll get, but you'll be getting paid more for your time.

There is also the 50/50 split. That's where an author will pay you 50% of the royalties of the audiobook for seven years. ACX handles the money, so you aren't going to get ripped off. This is what I did to get books under my belt, and some experience. I chose quick books, under an hour. I'm never going to make much money off them, but that wasn't the point.

If you do a split beyond just gaining experience, choose the books carefully. You want longer books, so the royalty is more than pennies. You also want books that are going to sell. ACX shows you the Amazon ranking of the books. Check them out, and any reviews. Check the author name for other books and see how well they've sold.

You want to make money for your work and agreeing to record a book that won't get many sales is a waste of time. Check out the audition text and see if it's been edited or has a ton of errors. Those won't sell well. They'll get returned with bad reviews. Don't touch them. Your time is money, and if you aren't going to get paid, you have a lot of other options in this book to work on until a good narrating opportunity arises.

In short, don't sell yourself cheap. Yeah, it's supposed to be "short," but I couldn't see me using "short" twice in the same sentence. Look what I just did.

. . .

Getting Your Books On ACX

Ok, you know how to produce an audiobook, so how do you do it without recording your own? ACX requires that your book be available on Amazon first. It can be paperback, eBook, or both. I don't know why, but that's the way they want it, and it's their sandbox. There is a safe way around this, and it will be discussed in the Going Wide chapter.

You'll need to log into ACX. Use your author account if you have a producer (narrator) account. You can't use the same email for a producer and author account. If you're narrating and publishing, you'll need two ACX accounts. On the top menu bar, next to your name, click on Projects, then Open for Auditions. There will be a purple "Assert more Titles" button on the right. Click that and fill in the fields. It will show you some books. Pick yours.

You'll need to decide how you're going to pay, either cold hard cash (PayPal) or a 50/50 split. If it's cash, how much? The more you're willing to pay, the higher quality narrators you'll attract. I strongly recommend you pay for production. Seven years is a long time to share profits. You'll also be waiting a long time for someone to accept a split if your book isn't doing too well on Amazon, or you're a first-time author. Narrators want to get paid. It's understandable.

You'll need an audition script too. Please use a .doc or .docx file. Text files and pdf's are horrible to work with. Choose a part of your book with difficult words to see how the narrators handle it. Even if they don't know the words, they should say them correctly – because the good ones will research how to pronounce them correctly. If they're words you made up, throw them a bone.

I speak some Russian – my wife is Ukrainian – and in my *Aftermath* books, I use some Russian words. I'm also from an area in Washington State with lots of Indian names. I use my state as the setting for the books. I didn't leave my narrator hanging, I recorded YouTube videos of me saying the words correctly. Give Puyallup a try. That's a word nobody gets right unless they live in the area. There is a video on YouTube of people trying, it's pretty funny. Sequim is another one nobody gets right. Know when to give your narrator help.

On my first book, I chose the narrator who got Elbe correct. I should have waited on that one. I didn't know any better and thought he had a good voice. The reviews have told me otherwise. The book sells well, but the narrator gets a lot of bad reviews. A lot. A lot, lot, lot. I didn't hire him for the other books. The new one is a gem, Warren Keyes. Look him up. While I do record my own now, I stayed with him for consistency. bit.ly/WarrenKeyes

Soon you'll start getting auditions. Listen to them carefully so you don't make the mistake I did on my first one. Let friends and family listen to them and see what they think. When you've found one you like, send them an offer. Include in your offer how much you're willing to pay or if you're offering a split. Then you wait.

If it's accepted, awesome! Send the narrator your full book file and sit back and wait. You've given due dates, so you know how long the wait will be. If you chose a split, be prepared to wait longer. Some narrators will put you behind paying jobs. Like I said, they want to get paid.

The narrator will record the first 15 minutes for you to approve or not. Listen to it and make sure it's what you want. If it's too fast, say something now. Don't wait until it's been completed. If there's anything you don't like, speak up. Now is not the time to be shy.

When the audiobook is done, you'll get an email. Log in and listen to the files. Listen to the whole book from start to finish. Listen for mistakes, like pops, clicks, and other noises. Make sure the volume is good and consistent throughout.

If everything sounds fine, approve the file, and contact the narrator for their PayPal email and pay them. If you did a split, you won't have that option. After you've sent payment, go back to the project file, and click the purple button, confirming you sent payment. Then the narrator will need to press the purple button on their side, confirming they received payment. Once that happens, ACX puts it in line, waiting for quality checks. It used to be about two weeks, but I've got some projects I completed six weeks ago still waiting to be approved.

If you read the narrator section, and I know you did because you rock, you already know ACX is going to pay you according to the length of your audiobook. A three-hour audiobook (29,100 words is the best bang for the buck. The next increase comes at 5 hours, or 48,500 words. After that, there isn't an increase in pay until a whopping ten hours, almost 100,000 words.

Books under three hours don't make very much per sale but can still add up. But you can turn three one-hour audiobooks into one three-hour audiobook. How? Simple, with a bundle! There are some rules with bundles on ACX.

You can only bundle an audiobook once, and they're strict about it. If you did a split, the same narrator must have recorded all the books in the bundle. If you paid for production, then who the narrators are doesn't matter. They will all need to be mentioned in the opening and closing credits, however.

You can ask one of the narrators to record the credits for you and offer to pay them $10 for their time. Use the ACX mail to communicate, but have the files sent to your email and pay via PayPal, of course.

You add the book to ACX as normal, but when it asks about the files, check the box that says you already have the files. You can download all the audiobook files from the Production tab. You'll need them, plus the opening and closing credits you had recorded for the bundle.

Then you start uploading all the files. It should go like this:

- Bundle opening credits in the Opening Credits slot.
- In the chapter slots, book 1 opening credits goes first
- Now all the chapters
- Book 1 closing credits
- Book 2 opening credits
- Book 2 chapters
- Book 2 closing credits
- Book 3 opening credits
- Book 3 chapters
- Book 3 closing credits
- Bundle closing credits in the Closing Credits slot
- Retail Audio Sample (choose one from one of the books or pay to have the description read.)

You can bundle as many books as you wish to get the three hours. Remember, it's better to have two three-hour audiobooks than one five or six-hour audiobook. You'll make more money.

Audiobooks are the future and are gaining popularity year after year. In today's publishing world, it really is a must to have audiobook versions of all your books, except cookbooks. They don't do very well in audio, understandably so.

THE GAME CHANGER

Not many people know this, but you can offer a downloadable pdf to all your audiobook listeners. But Kevin, what am I supposed to put in a pdf? Why would they care? Those are great questions! You ask a lot of great questions; inquisitive minds go far.

You put together some extra information that deals with the same subject as the audiobook. It can be a report (plr is good for this), checklist, the photos in the book, anything. Photos are great; they're in your book because they help the reader. But so far, the technology doesn't exist to see them in audio. That would be a great day. So, put them in a separate Word file with the other information I'll tell you about, and export as pdf.

In a book, we can put links for the reader to use. In audio, we have to say the links. Most times, the listener isn't going to be able to write them down, so provide them in your pdf.

If you've got an email list for this book, put that link in the pdf. Ask them to sign up and tell them the benefits of being on your list. Don't be shy. Most of the writers I know are introverts, myself included, but you must put yourself out there for repeat customers. Don't be afraid to ask for subscribers or reviews.

Which brings me to the last point – you have another opportunity to ask for a review. Don't let it slide by. The good thing about Audible reviews is friends and family are permitted to leave reviews. They need to purchase the audiobook to leave a review, however. But no worries, ACX gives you promotional codes to giveaway for free copies. Use them. Use them all. Ask for reviews for the freebies.

So you have your content, your links, email signup, and review request all set. Create the pdf and email ACX at support@acx.com after the book has been approved by you and paid for. Let them know you have a pdf available for download after purchase. That's important. Pdf's are also available before purchase. You don't want that. Attach the pdf and send it. Include the book title and author name.

One last thing, when you write your description for the audiobook, make sure you mention the free pdf download available after purchase. It will be in their library. ACX descriptions are much shorter than Amazon allows, so you may have to rewrite it for ACX.

Chapter 6 Exercise

Open an ACX account, either for author or producer (narrator.) If you're going to do both, then open two accounts, using two different email addresses. For authors only, that's about all you can do until you get a book completed. But that's ok, you'll be ready to rock.

For narrators, open your account and get some practice reading and editing done using public domain books. When you get a track you like, add it to your profile. Every time you put a new sample in your account, ACX moves you to the top of the search results, so you can pick up some work easier.

CHAPTER 7 A NEW WAY FOR AFFILIATE MARKETING

I told myself there wouldn't be any affiliate marketing in this book. But then I realized a lot of readers would be affiliate marketers or had tried and fallen for the lies. I also said I'd be telling all my secrets, so I couldn't leave this out.

I still use YouTube for affiliate marketing. I'd be foolish to leave that untapped. But I make much more money with my own way. Putting affiliate links in books is nothing new; most people do it. There are some in this book. That is expected.

But if you want to really sell your affiliate product, you need to write a book *around* the product. What does that mean? Let's say you signed up for an account at Clickbank and want to be an affiliate for *His Secret Obsession*. I just looked this one up, and it seems like a good one to promote. It's in Self-Help which is a huge niche and one people spend money on.

Their affiliate page says it's helped thousands of women improve their relationships. It teaches women how to tap into a man's desire. Whatever that is. I don't have any secret desires. I feel left out. Anyway, it's teaching women how to love and be loved, it seems.

What you would do is hit the relationship forums to do your book research. You can use scholar.google.com to look up studies too. Look at other relationship books on Amazon, check out their reviews. Do everything I told you about earlier. Then start writing.

Books like these don't need to be long. You can do a short read or knock out 10,000 words. Don't charge a premium for shorter books though. For 10k words, I wouldn't go above $12.99. But that's ok. You're counting on your affiliate product to make money. So, you can sell your books cheaper and maybe get more readers.

There is one thing to keep in mind while writing these types of books: Don't make it look like an advertisement. People aren't stupid. They will see right through it. In this example, you would write a book about keeping relationships strong, or rekindling a marriage that has become too quiet. Anything along those lines, use your research to figure it out.

You'll only mention your product a few times. Soft sell it. Say what it does, give the benefits, and move on. For those who sign up to your email list, you can talk about it in an email too. Since most people need to see an offer seven times before making a purchase, it's a good idea to ask them to sign up to your email list.

You'll ask them to sign up to be notified of future books and offer them a free report upon signup. Find some PLR dealing with relationship advice for your report. You can offer it as a download if you have the capability, or just send it in an email – several emails if it's a long report. You can space them out every five or seven days. Sooner too, if you wish.

You can make an army of short reads with these types of books. I wouldn't go too short, maybe around an hour would be good, 8-10,000 words. It may sound like a lot, but it's not. That's an easy book to write. You could get away with shorter books if you must. I wouldn't go below 30 minutes, however. Remember to let people know it's a short read in the description. "In this short book, you'll discover…"

Clickbank has a lot of products, and they're organized by niche. That's a huge help to you. It will help make a niche specific army of books. You can keep them all on one email list. Repeat buyers are your friend. Repeat buyers leave reviews too.

Most marketers in the IM field are bad actors. One of them I trust is the best **PLR** writer in the business, Arun Chandrun. Once a year, he writes reviews of the top selling Clickbank products, and it's a huge seller. He just released his Clickbank 2020 reviews, and they're awesome. kevinbarrymaguire.com/Click-bank-2020

Most of the people buying them won't do much, if anything, with them. The rest will be selling them on their websites and/or YouTube. Let them and join them. Don't let an income stream go to waste. I have video reviews up of all his reviews. They're on my prepper website too. But selling in books beats them all.

Remember, you can't use **PLR** for books on Amazon. They will terminate your account. But you use them as an outline. Arun has already done the product research. He's given you the plusses and minuses. All you need to do is write around it.

Then, you can put the whole review on your website or blog. You can even use a free blog, like Blogger.com. And if you know how to make videos, you can make a video using the **PLR**. Change up some words so Google approves. They don't like identical content. So use it mostly as is, but make it your own.

Another of the good guys is Steve Chase. Steve is a professional voiceover guy and has turned Arun's Clickbank articles into videos each year - kevinbarrymaguire.com/CB-Videos. Can you guess how I got all my videos done? Yep. I bought Steve's. I can make videos myself, but it takes time. I buy them to save me time that I can spend elsewhere. Time is money.

When you upload the videos to YouTube, put a link in the first line of the description pointing to your blog post. Do not point directly to the product page. YouTube will zap you with a strike or just delete your channel on the first offense. They have no standards for it. One strike can get you deleted, or three strikes can. Three will every time.

From your blog post, you can either send them to a squeeze page for an email address or send them to the offer page. Email is king. You should have a good offer if you're going to ask for their email. Some Clickbank offers have affiliate pages, and on those pages, you can find free reports for your email campaigns. Not all of them will have that, but it's worth a look.

You can also send people to your book from your blog. If you have a Word Press website, you can get the Pretty Links plugin. That's awesome. You can use Pretty Links in YouTube descriptions, so you can point people to your book from the video. Pretty Links is worth having a website for by itself.

Pretty Links works like bit.ly but is much more professional looking. You paste in the destination link, then create words for the end of the link. For instance, for Dale L Roberts' free Startup Guide, the link looks like this: kevinbarrymaguire.com/Dales-Startup

It's my website with "Dales-Startup" at the end. The link goes to my website and forwards to Dale's. The actual link is long and unruly. Pretty Links cleans it up and makes it professional. It has the added benefit of hiding the affiliate information.

Why would I want to do that if I tell them it's an affiliate link? You do have to tell them, by the way. It's the law. Some people don't like affiliate links, thinking it will cost them extra. They attempt to remove the affiliate portion of the link. Then all your hard work doesn't get rewarded.

Using affiliate links doesn't cost the buyer extra, of course. A lot of affiliate links offer a discount, but none charge more for using them. A few of my links will save you money if you use them. You'll get the added privilege of knowing you helped feed my daughter and her cat too.

The goal of the book is to get people on your list and to the Clickbank offer. The goal of video is to get them to your blog and/or book. The goal of the blog is to get people to a squeeze page, the offer, and/or your book. You have a three-pronged attack, and they're all cross-promoting. It's powerful.

Chapter 7 Exercise

You've probably guessed where I'm going with this by now. You're going to create an account at Clickbank.com and find something you'd like to promote. Then research your niche, make an outline, and write a short read dealing with the subject. I'll make it easy and say only 6,000-8,000 words. No sweat.

CHAPTER 8 WRITING COPY

This is the most important part of anything you do online. What is copy? It's your book description, product description, titles, subtitles, and bullet points in Merch by Amazon. It's the words you use to persuade people to buy what you're selling.

Book covers grab attention and get people to take a closer look. But the description sells the book. T-shirts could be an exception. People buy them for how they look. The bullet points help but are mostly for keywords. Different products require different tactics, but writing copy is generally the same for everything.

Does it work? Like a charm. If you write a description off the top of your head and one that you researched and used copywriting techniques, you will get many more sales with the second one. Good copywriters make a lot of money. It's something to investigate if you become proficient at it. It's another way to make money online, although, it's not a passive income.

Fiction Copy

Just like writing fiction, writing fiction copy can be fun. I start off with a question or a short statement. In my first *Aftermath* book, the description starts off with, "Could you survive a post-apocalyptic world?" It's in bold so it stands out and should be larger text. I need to go back and fix that.

Amazon only gives a few lines before "read more" shows up. I use larger text, so my first line is all they see. I want them to click "read more." It means they're interested. I've piqued their curiosity. That Book 1 description was the first one I wrote, and I knew very little about copywriting. I knew to ask a question at the start. We all start somewhere.

Your first three or four lines should be six words or less and double space the lines. Yes, mine is seven. Exceptions to every rule, that hyphenation must be an exception. If I were re-writing the description today, it would look something like this:

Could you survive a post-apocalyptic world?

The day starts like any other.

Then disaster strikes.

Jack's lifetime of preparing will be put to the test. He grabbed his dogs, his girlfriend, and their bugout bags - and got out of dodge.

The duo must escape to Jack's cottage near Mt. Rainier. Will they make it in time?

*Survival is for the prepared. Scroll up and **buy now**.*

I may have to use this one. It looks nothing like the original one. The purpose of double spacing the lines is to keep the readers eyes moving down. You want them to reach the call to action. It also reads like there is action. If you haven't noticed, authors use short sentences in action scenes. It simulates speed and action.

I kept my use of bold to a minimum because the description is so short. Fiction descriptions don't need to be long and drawn out. Short and simple does the trick. Because the quote text above is in italics, I couldn't use any in showing this. If I use this description, I will use italics for "disaster." That's about all the formatting I would do here. In a longer description, I'd use bold instead. But you can't overdo bold, it looks bad. When you do use it, bold action words.

In the original description, I used both main character's names, "Jack and Diane." But one of the books I read on writing fiction descriptions said to only use one name, and then only the first name. It was a different book that talked about short sentences and double spacing. I got a lot out of that one; it's called, "Mastering Amazon Descriptions: An Author's Guide: Copywriting for Authors," by Brian D Meeks.

There is only one non-fiction example in the whole book. Some of what he says works for nonfiction. If you're writing fiction, this is a must-read. If you're writing nonfiction, you should read it and use what you can for your descriptions.

There needs to be a goal; what is the main character trying to do? What event started the quest? Explain both in a few sentences, don't write an article. You want readers wanting more; you aren't giving away the farm here.

It will take a little practice, but once you get the hang of it, it's no problem. I think the hardest part is the first line. Will you use a statement or a question? That's the easy part. Coming up with the words is the hard part.

One thing, you aren't supposed to ask questions with yes/no answers, so it looks like I need to work on mine still. You don't want the potential customer to say, "no" and move on to the next book. A better question for me would be, "What would you do to survive?" or "How would you survive?" But then I'd have to throw in post-apocalyptic somewhere else.

If I were to use a statement, I might just say, "Disaster" or "Disaster struck." Next line. Maybe even, "It happened." The reaction you want from the reader is, "What? What comes next?" You need to hook them. The longer they read, the more likely they are to purchase.

. . .

Nonfiction Copy

Does it work?

You bought this book, didn't you? Why? Was it the cover that made you decide? The title or subtitle? Or did the description convince you that this was the book you were looking for? Odds are, it was the description.

Nonfiction follows the same basic rules as fiction. The first three to four lines will look the same. But after that, everything changes. Ask your question or make your opening statement. Hook them. Then write a few lines to keep their eyes moving. Double spaced. Then a paragraph or two followed by short sentences and double spacing.

In the middle or bottom, you'll need a bulleted list of stuff you discuss in the book. Most people introduce the list with something like, "In this book you will learn." Most people are *wrong*. Learning sounds like school, or homework. Don't use that word. Instead, you write, "In this book you will discover." Discover is much cooler; it's like an adventure. People like adventure.

At the bottom of the list, either in the last bullet or under the list, write, "And much more. Make it bold. Don't use an exclamation point. Keep those to a bare minimum if you must use one. But don't use them. You'll start to sound like a used car salesman, and it's game over.

At the bottom, you'll of course have your call to action because you aren't shy, and you know it brings you more sales. Something as simple as "Scroll up and click '**Buy Now**'" will work. For this book, I will probably say something like, "Scroll up and click '**Buy Now**' to start earning today." I don't know yet. I haven't even thought of a title yet. I don't write the description until I've finished the book, but for this one, I'll be writing it in this chapter. That should be fun.

So how are you going to fill the space above the bullet list? You're going to study your audience. I know my audience because I am the audience. I'm in the Facebook groups and engage people. I'm a moderator in Dale's Facebook group - bit.-ly/Dales-Group. (Answer all three questions, or you'll be denied. You can tell the truth. It's ok if you've never watched Dale or Kelli.) I watch the best YouTube channels, you've seen them by now – Dale, Julie, Keith, Jacob, Walter, and Ryan. I won't have to research. It's one of the many benefits of writing what you know.

Where do you find your audience? Message boards still exist, strange as it seems. Those are great places to learn your audience. Posts are saved and easy to search. You can see how many times the post was read, showing you its popularity. You can instantly see the hot topics.

What are you looking for? Pain points. What does your audience need and can't find a solution to? What solutions aren't working? What is working? If it's working and not in your book, get it in there. What do they wish they had? Find out what they can't do without. You want to know every little detail about your audience.

If you're writing a weight loss book, you can say, "How many times have you dieted and not seen results?" "Do you want to fit in your jeans this summer?" You'd ask that because someone said it in a forum post. That post had a lot of engagement. Someone said, "I'm trying to lose weight so my jeans will fit in the summer." It's as easy as that.

You can also use Facebook groups, but they aren't as good. You can search group posts, but the search feature needs work. I've searched for my own posts in groups and can't find them. You're going to see only the newest posts, for the most part. But it can't hurt to look. You could find a gem.

Another place you're going to check has already been discussed – Amazon reviews. Look at books in your niche and read the reviews, good and bad. This should have been done already, when researching your book, so you should know what is missing from the other books and put it in yours.

You'll be able to say, "Most books don't touch [this topic], but in [book title] you will discover how to…" Just make sure it's true. Don't lie in your description. A lie may gain you a few sales, but it will also come with bad reviews. If the lie is bad enough, Amazon could take action. You don't want that.

You aren't solving their problems in the description; you're only confirming them. You're making them say, "Yes." Yes is good. On a side note, a word you should use a few times is "by." Why? Because it sounds like "buy," and that's another word you want in their heads.

There are more words you should be using in your copy. What is the most powerful word in copywriting? You. Use it a lot. You can also use "your." Those words personalize the copy to the audience. "Now" is a word that creates a sense of urgency and is great in your call to action. "Limited" works in the same way.

Discover. It's a powerful word, as discussed earlier. Did you notice I used it above, outside of a bullet list? Powerful. It is a word that is, well… powerful in copywriting. If something is powerful, people want it. Immediately. We live in a "gotta have it now" society. People are impatient.

I saw a guy complaining about a PLR writer in his Facebook group. The guy was angry because it took two months to make money from his PLR. Two months. He wasn't angry because he was making money; he was angry that it took two months. I was speechless. That doesn't happen often.

Back to the power words… More. People always want more. New. A shiny, new car, a new iPhone, new anything. Do you have a new way to solve someone's problem? In the bullet list, you can write, "New system revolutionizes your [problem.]" Again, don't give away the answer. If they can read the answer in the description, they don't need your book.

Today. It goes with "immediately." How to. "How to…" is searched a lot because people are looking for how to do things. They want their problems solved. Your books show them.

Secret. I've got a secret. Now there is a Styx song in my head.

Everyone wants to know secrets. You will spark the reader's curiosity with this word. Again, don't use the word if it isn't true. You can't just claim a secret to use the word. You're putting out quality. Quality always wins.

Best. It's a good word, but it's also one Amazon doesn't like you to use, so it's best not to use it. Yes, the pun was intended. It's who I am. It's what I do.

There are a lot more words, and you can see the whole list at bit.ly/Copy-Power-Words. Be careful with a few of those words. Amazon doesn't like misleading words, like best.

Now I'll write my description. But note, since my book isn't finished yet, there will probably be changes to the final version. It will probably look similar to this, but not exactly.

You've been lied to.

You believed them.

And they lied.

How many times have you bought that pushbutton software that **promised** $267.35 at the push of a button? They promised free traffic built in. You believed it. Why would they lie?

You **waited** for the next email, the one that would *finally* show you the easy way to make money online. You read the sales page. The testimonials *praising* the product. A few of the "customers" probably looked familiar. But they all lied.

You know they lied.

. . .

Because you bought it again.

Are you tired of the dirty "Make money online" world? Are you tired of the unethical marketers? Are you **ready** to learn how it's really done? I don't give you a button to press for $375.95 instantly.

You will discover the many ways I found to make **honest** money online. Without affiliates. Without buttons. Without lies.

By the time you finish this book, you will discover:

- How to write books that sell, without words
- How to write 5-page books that sell, over and over
- How to turn your voice into money
- How you, yes you, can write nonfiction
- How to turn Photoshop or Gimp into a cash machine
- Turn your camera into a money-maker
- How to sell a book you didn't write, legally
- A new way to sell affiliate products, buh bye video
- **And more!**

I've been sold the lies internet marketers tell. I've *waited* for those emails. I spent a few grand learning that you can't make money with their push-button software. The marketers make the money, your money. You only lose money.

It took me about a year and a few thousand dollars to learn how to make money online, the **right** way. In this book, I'll show you how. Some ways are fast; some are slow, but they all create an income stream.

If you want to earn a little extra money to save or have fun, you need this book. If you want to make enough money to quit your job and work at home, you need this book.

Discover how I did it. Scroll up and click "**Buy Now**" today and get started.

Ok, that was fun. That was right off the top of my head. But I know the audience. Everything I said there was true. That money wasted would have been another thousand dollars, but I was able to get my money back from that one. The Internet Marketing world is full of bad actors. Unfortunately, some of them migrated over to publishing.

But don't worry about them for now. I won't be referring to any of them. If you see a software that I haven't mentioned, ask yourself why. There may be a good reason. Ask in a Facebook group if the software is safe. I'll give you a hint, the mass uploaders are bad. Very bad. They have done a lot of damage to no and low-content publishing.

Enough with the downer talk. Notice how I used the power words in my description. I used "discover" three times. "You" and "how to" are used a lot. I also hit the pain points hard because I know exactly how they feel. I also know you can't push a button and have money come pouring in, unless you're at an ATM, and you have money in the bank.

I didn't overdo the bold and added italics between. You do that to keep their eyes busy. It keeps interest, just like the short sentences and short paragraphs. Whatever you do, do not use a big block of paragraphs. People will tune out in a hurry. TLDR is a thing – To Long, Didn't Read. If they aren't reading, they aren't buying.

That applies to everything you do online. Websites, emails, Facebook posts, anything. If you write long paragraphs, most people aren't going to read them. I also keep that in mind when

I'm writing books. I allow very few paragraphs to go on for too long.

Merch Copy

Merch copywriting is much easier than the previous items. You have your title and two bullet points. That's it. You have room for a description, but most people leave it blank. It's not used by Amazon for keywords, only Google. I copy my descriptive bullet point and paste it into that field.

Your title needs to be descriptive and have keywords in it. You don't put shirt, t-shirt, or tee in the titles. We used to, but now Amazon does it for us, which is cool. It gives us more room for our titles. The same applies to all the other types of tops you can sell. Sweatshirts, hoodies, etc.

So, if I'm making a birthday shirt for a seven-year old boy, I might have a race car on the shirt with "Happy birthday." A "7" or "7th" would need to be there too. "Happy 7th Birthday" would work for this example. The car could go below the words. You might even be able to fit a balloon.

My title would read: "Happy 7th Birthday Boy Shirt with Red Race Car"

I used "shirt" in the title because I used the search bar to find out what people were searching for. Amazon's suggestions told me they are searching for "Happy 7th Birthday Boy Shirt." It's going to look funny because Amazon is still going to add "T-Shirt" at the end. It will look like I wrote it. The listing is going to read:

Happy 7th Birthday Boy Shirt with Red Race Car T-shirt

It looks goofy, but sometimes it's unavoidable. I'd rather not use "shirt," but I wanted the whole phrase in order. Most people aren't reading the titles, however. They're looking at the shirt and making a quick decision.

Describe colors if you can, people search them – especially on PopSockets. They want to match the PopSocket color with their phone. Amazon wants you to describe your shirt (or PopSocket) in the title. Just the shirt. What it says or what any illustrations are. Don't use anything misleading; they don't like that at all.

Amazon doesn't allow words such as glitter, neon, gold, or metallic in titles or descriptions. It takes special equipment for them to show up correctly on shirts and PopSockets. If you use those words, you'll get a rejection for "Inaccurate Product Descriptions."

The bullet points are where people tend to keyword stuff. Amazon says they don't like keyword stuffing, but a lot of the top ranked shirts do it. I don't do it, but I get enough in there. In the first line, I'll write something like this:

Our design is a great birthday gift idea. Great present for family, friends, kids, boys, nephew, grandson.

The keywords are there, somewhat stuffed. I've seen a lot worse – on the top ranked shirts. The second line describes the shirt again.

Surprise your friends or family with this popular trending tee. A perfect gift for your child and your friend's children. Design features white text, "Happy 7th Birthday" with a bright red race car and blue balloon.

Here I can add more descriptor words than in the title. Since I didn't actually make this design, I don't know if I'd use other colors for the text, so basic white works for this example.

FYI, I won't be making this design, so feel free to use it. Remember to change things so there aren't multiple versions of it. I have a backlog of designs waiting to be uploaded already. I also didn't do any of the trademark research. You will have to do that if you use this example.

The last place for your keywords is the Brand Name. You'll need to trademark check your brand names too. I would try something like, "Birthday Shirts for Boys by Amy." I would trade-mark check, "Birthday Shirts for Boys" then add "by Amy" when listing it.

Why would I add the name? Because someone else might use the same name, but they won't think of adding "by" to it. So, your brand won't get mixed up with theirs. You can share your brand name. When you do, you don't want shirts from other people showing up. I use a female name 99% of the time. I never looked up the stats, but since most shoppers are women, it makes sense to use a woman's name.

That's all there is to writing copy for Merch. Every other type discussed here is easy enough to figure out and is more like Merch than book descriptions.

Chapter 8 Exercise

If you have a book written already, write a description for it. Use those powerful words I gave you. If you haven't written one, think of one you'd like to write and create the description for it. You'll need to do the research to learn the pain points first, but no worries, you'll have than knocked out for when you're ready to write.

CHAPTER 9 AMAZON ADS

There's no magic science to running ads for your book. A good cover, a good title and good sales copy will carry you far. There is no secret recipe.

Jacob Rothenberg The Publishing Evolution
kevinbarrymaguire.com/Publishing-Evolution

---

*T*see this question a lot in Facebook groups: What is the best way to advertise my book? There is one simple answer: Amazon Ads. Your buyers are already there; they're actively searching for books (or shirt and educational products) to buy. They are buyers – the best kind of traffic. I don't advertise anywhere else. Nobody else has the built-in buyer traffic.

Some people use Facebook ads as well. Most people get taken to the cleaners, from what I've seen in Facebook groups. I don't recommend starting out with Facebook ads. You'll need to be on the top of your game before going that route. I would watch all the YouTube videos I could, and maybe even take a course on Facebook ads before giving it a try.

As it stands with the topics I discuss, Amazon is only giving ads to KDP and Merch. Merch ads are closed to new accounts for the time being. I don't know why. They opened them up a little over a year ago, then shut out any new ad accounts after a few months.

When your account was eligible, Amazon gave a code you were to use to open the account. A lot of people put it off and got shut out. So, if you see the code in your account, don't wait. Jump on it immediately. If you're in Facebook groups, you'll know when ads open up again. It will be the talk of social media.

KDP Ads

I'll start with ads for KDP because they're always open. The first thing you need to do is go to www.ads.amazon.com and open up an account. It's all the normal stuff: name, address, phone, and credit or debit card info.

To create your first ad, click the yellowish orangish button on the left. It says, "Create campaign." It will take you to a page to make a choice, sponsored products or lockscreen ads. Choose sponsored products. Everyone I know who has used lockscreen ads has been disappointed. A few of them are ad experts. I took their advice and have stayed away from them.

At the top, give your campaign a name, something easy to remember. If you're creating an ad for a journal for women, call it "Journal for Women." Simple wins the day. The start date will already be filled out, so don't change it unless you really want it to start later. I always leave the end date at the default – no end date. If I want to stop it, I can do that any time I need to, manually.

Daily budget. You can put whatever you want but show Amazon you're serious and put at least $5.00 in that slot. The odds are very slim you'll get near that $5.00 in normal times. I've only hit the limit with one book, and it hit every day from sometime in November to December 22nd – ish. The awesome Q4. I let it run to the limit every day. For a while, I raised it. I was making a killing with that book and saw no reason not to let it run.

There is one thing you must keep in mind: Amazon charges your ads every month. When you're new, they ding you at milestones, so when you spend $50 in ads, they'll ding you immediately. Then $100, etc. I don't know the exact amounts, just make sure you can cover it.

While they charge you monthly, the money you make from selling the books won't show up into your account for about three months. Remember, Amazon pays two months after the month of the sale… at the end of the second month. So, it's about three months.

The good news is, I have about 50 ads running at any given time and they all have $5.00 daily limits. My ad bill runs between $50 and $100 a month, very few ads go over a dollar a day, and not for long. Unless, of course, it's Q4. During Q4, you need to be very careful. Ad spend will go up dramatically. So will the money you make. You just won't see it until around February 27th. But you will see the bill a lot sooner. You should check in on your ads every day, twice during Q4.

Targeting has two phases. At first, you'll choose Automatic. Every two weeks, download the csv file that shows which keywords you're getting charged for. You want to scan for the ones that are working. Write them down in Notepad. Then you'll start a Manual Targeting campaign, using only the keywords that have been working.

For the Campaign bidding strategy, I always choose "Dynamic bids – down only." So, if I can win an ad placement with a smaller bid, that's what I'll be charged. "Up and down" means they'll go above your bid if it will win you the ad placement. That seems dangerous to me. Fixed bids mean if you bid 20 cents, that's what you'll be charged.

Ad Format. If you choose to do a custom ad, you'll write custom text for viewers to read. If you've got a catchy tag line, this is where you'd put it. They can be frustrating, however. Amazon is very picky about what you put in there. Like, the title must match perfectly: word for word, upper case and lower case, italic, etc. It must all match.

Standard ads, on the other hand, are a piece of cotton candy. What, you were expecting cake? Amazon just shows your cover and title. A lot of times, that's enough. Readers do, in fact, judge books by their covers. So, if your cover is awesome, that could be enough. If your cover needs work, you may want to write a catchy tagline and go with a custom ad.

Products. This one is simple. Find your book and click the Add button. You can't overthink this one.

Default Bid. Don't use Amazon's suggested bid. It's way too high. Start at 12 cents and see what happens. If you aren't getting impressions, raise it up. For me, I start my bids at 20 cents now. You are bidding against others for the same keywords. Highest bid wins. If you want the first page of results, at the top, you'll be paying much more than 20 cents. In Romance, you're looking at $1 per click minimum to get that coveted spot. You're paying per click, not impression.

For our low bids, we're going to be on page two or farther most times. It still works. To get on the first page, you'll need to increase the price of your book. Otherwise, you'll be spending more than you make. If you're advertising a $6.99 notebook, you must keep your bids low if you plan to see a profit.

Negative keywords. If you have a keyword you don't want Amazon to target, you would list it here. The only example I have is a Keto book of mine. Automatic targeting was going after vegan keywords. Those don't do me any good with Keto, so I would list those words in that box.

If you chose manual targeting, then the negative box would be replaced with Keyword Targeting. You'll see a Bid line and a gray box that defaults to Suggested Bid. You don't want that. Change it to Custom Bid and enter your bid amount.

Under that, uncheck "Phrase" and "Exact." Then you will see some suggested keywords. Go ahead and add what you like. Above the bid type box, you'll see Related, Enter List, and Upload File. Enter list is where you would enter your keyword list manually. Either by typing it in or doing a copy/paste.

Upload file is if you have a csv file ready to go. If you have Publisher Rocket, you can do your keyword research there in a few seconds, and download the csv file of your completed list. Then upload that file to Amazon Ads via this tab. The time Publisher Rocket saves you in looking for keywords is priceless - kevinbarrymaguire.com/Publisher-Rocket.

Rocket will find keywords you'd never even consider. Don't remove them. I saw one for my Keto book that made me laugh. But it was my second-best keyword! It made me a lot of money. This has happened to others too. Dale L Roberts told me a few stories where it happened to him.

Ok, you'll see Negative keywords again, but skip it. You won't need them because you're entering all the keywords in. You aren't going to enter keywords you don't want; I assume. All that is left is to click that Launch campaign button on the bottom right. Then wait a few hours for approval, then a few days for the impressions to start showing.

Some tips. If you only have a few impressions after about a week, your bid is too low. If you have a lot of impressions but few or no clicks, your cover needs work. If you have a lot of clicks but no buys, your description needs work. Your cover attracts buyers, the description sells the book. I may or may not repeat that again.

For manual targeting, find a lot of keywords. Amazon gives you 1,000 per ad. If you have more than 1,000, then make another ad. It is very difficult to hit those numbers without the aid of software. If you did automatic targeting first, then only use the profitable keywords from the ad.

If you've spent more than your profit from one sale, kill the ad. It's not working. If I have an ad on a $6.99 notebook and the ad has cost me two dollars without a sale, I stop the ad and don't look back. Two dollars is what I would have made on a sale.

It has happened to me on several occasions. The only thing you can do is forget ads on that book altogether or fix the description. When people are clicking and not buying, they didn't like your description.

However, sales do take a while to show up in the report. On your KDP dashboard, sales only show up when the book has been shipped. You won't know when someone bought a book, only when it's been shipped. Nobody knows what takes so long for sales to show up in your ads reports. So, after you stop an ad, check in on it after a week or two and see if any sales showed up. If they did, and you're ok with the cost, then start it up again. Otherwise, forget about it.

Dave Chesson has a free Amazon Ads course you can find here: https://kevinbarrymaguire.com/AMS-Course

Merch Ads

Merch is about the same as KDP. You can get away with smaller bids in a lot of niches. You'll use the same $5.00 max spend daily, and never come close to reaching it.

With automatic targeting, make sure your title and bullet points are spot on. Amazon will use those to determine the keywords for your ad. What that means to you is don't put irrelevant keywords in your listing. Relevant keywords only. That should be for everything you do on Amazon. But in this case, it will save you money.

If you use keywords that have nothing to do with your shirt or PopSocket, Amazon will try to advertise those keywords.

You're going to end up with clicks without sales. You're paying for each click, remember.

If I'm looking for a 10th birthday shirt for my daughter, and I click on your ad but only see an engineering shirt, I'm not buying it. Most people won't. People on Amazon usually know what they want. Using correct keywords will help them and you. They find what they're looking for, you get a sale.

Once again, keep a sharp eye on your ads. Keep two sharp eyes on them in Q4. I had a shirt crank out a $30 cost and no sales. I'd had a problem logging into my ads account and kept putting off contacting Amazon. That was not very smart of me. The shock was hard on my system when I finally logged back in.

It was a Christmas shirt that I thought looked pretty cool. A lot of others did too, but something kept them from making the purchase. I never did figure out what that was. It was also my first Q4, and I had no idea what it did to ads. So now you know, and you know why I say "keep two eyes" on your ads during Q4.

Chapter 9 Exercise

Get over to Amazon Ads and create an account. Until you have a book live on Amazon, that's all you can do. If you do have at least one live, decide whether or not you're going to advertise. If not, you're done with the exercise. I'm not going to tell anyone to start an ad. That's a decision only you can make.

If you are going to advertise, then you have another decision – automatic or not. Since this is your first ad, however, you may want to choose auto. Fill out the rest and let her rip!

CHAPTER 10 GOING WIDE

MARKETING & PROMOTION

One of the best ways to connect with your ideal reader is through video. It's often free and accessible for both you and your ideal reader. To build an unstoppable author brand, break ground in video right away.

Dale L Roberts

kevinbarrymaguire.com/Dales-Startup

What is "going wide?" You've asked another fine question. When you're only on Amazon, you've got your entire income stream in one place. It's a good place with a lot of native traffic, but anything can happen. If that something is bad, you're out of an income stream.

Going wide means taking your stuff to other platforms as well. It's like diversifying your portfolio in the stock market world. You will still have everything on Amazon, but now you'll have it all over the place. You'll make the most money with Amazon but can come close or exceed the Amazon money with everything else combined. So, if anything happens to your Amazon account, you've got a backup.

You should wait until you're comfortable on Amazon, however. Get your feet wet, learn the ropes, then go wide. When you're ready, go everywhere that takes your products and open an account and start posting.

For eBooks, you need to make sure you aren't in KDP Select. If you entered that program to get the page reads, then you'll have to opt out before going wide. KDP Select runs on 90-day contracts and auto-renews. To opt out, go to your bookshelf and find the eBook or eBooks you want to go wide with, and look for the "Promote and Advertise" button. Next to it, you'll see another button with an ellipse, or three dots. Hover over that, and you'll see a menu. Choose "KDP Select Info," and you can opt out when you get to the page.

You will have to wait until the three months are up, and it will tell you when that is. Or you can email KDP and ask to be removed early. That comes at a cost, however. You will lose all money made from the start of the current 90-day period for that book. If you've made good money since the start of the 90-day period, wait it out.

So, where can you go? It depends on what you're going wide with. Some only take eBooks; some will take paperback and eBook. There are a lot of places to go wide with t-shirts and a few places for audiobooks. In the next chapter, Stock Photography and Illustrations, you'll be going wide from the start.

eBooks

You can go to Google Play Books, Barnes & Noble Press, iBooks Author (app), Kobo, and a few others. You open accounts in each and upload your books to each one. Booooriiing.

Or... you can use an aggregator and only upload the book once. Those are places like Draft2Digital.com, Publish Drive.-

com, or IngramSpark.com. I used to use PublishDrive, but they started charging for each upload. So now it's Draft2Digital. Ingram is a great choice, but they charge per upload, and it isn't cheap.

There is a way around the upload fee for IngramSpark, however. If you become a member of the Alliance of Independent Authors (ALLi), you get all your Ingram upload fees waived - bit.ly/Member-ALLi. Ingram charges $49 for a print book and eBook, ALLi is $119 per year if you have one or more books. When you've been at this a while it increases to $149 per year if you're making your living from self-publishing. It's a bargain if you're going to use Ingram. An eBook alone is $25, and a print book alone is still $49.

I have not used IngramSpark for an eBook yet, but I plan on it. I have used them for several print books and will be scaling that up soon. Right after I join ALLi myself. Cutting out that fee makes it a no-brainer.

These aggregators get paid by taking a small percentage of your profit. It's a small price to pay for not having to take the time to upload to a bunch of different platforms, and it is the only way to get into libraries. There is one exception, Google Play Books - play.google.com/books. Almost a year ago, they stopped accepting uploads from aggregators unless the author had an account at Google Play Books.

It's been a pain in the rump for me. I was doing very well on Google until they made this rule. I applied immediately and still have not been accepted. So, all my books are off Google. After Amazon, Google gave me the most sales. Then Barnes & Noble.

I tried putting my fiction books wide for a while but have pulled them back and put them back in KDP Select. It took about three months before everyone took my book out of circulation. Get confirmation before going back to KDP Select. Amazon gets upset when you have your eBook somewhere else while you're enrolled in Select.

. . .

Print Books

Where Attention Goes, Income Flows
Dale L Roberts

You don't have many options for going wide with your paperbacks. You have IngramSpark, of course. Your only remaining option for now is Draft2Digital. Their paperback option is still in beta. PublishDrive has been teasing a print option for about six months, maybe longer.

If you want your books in bookstores, you're going to need to go with IngramSpark. They can also get you into libraries. If you search around the Internet, you can find coupons to waive the upload fee at Ingram. But if you're going to upload a lot of books, you will be better off joining ALLi and getting all your uploads free – eBook and paperback.

IngramSpark has strict guidelines for your pdf uploads, both for your cover and your interior. I have found that Word and PowerPoint do not cut the mustard. All my files from those programs were rejected no matter what I tried.

What works? Adobe Acrobat Pro and Vellum have worked for me. I have an old version of Acrobat, and it's flaking out on me now. No updates are available anymore. Adobe wants me to pay monthly for something I already bought. Nope. I use Vellum - kevinbarrymaguire.com/Vellum - to format everything.

I'll be doing the paperback cover for this book in Designer, so when I send it to IngramSpark, I'll know if Affinity products work there. I assume all of Adobe's products will work, being that Acrobat does. I used Photoshop for a cover before, and it works.

T-Shirts

There are a lot of places on the Internet to sell your t-shirts. The most common ones are Teespring, TeePublic, RedBubble, Café Press, Zazzle, Sun Frog, Gear Bubble, and Printful. There are many more.

The only ones I've used are Teespring and RedBubble, with minimal results. I'm told by Dale and Kelli Roberts that stickers sell better on RedBubble. At RedBubble and a few of the others, you can put your design on a variety of products. I did try Café Press when it first opened online, but it was so many years ago that I can't say what it's like today. They do have more than shirts, however.

Kelli Roberts has tried Zazzle but didn't like the experience. I'm comfortable sticking with just Merch for now. I still have my accounts at TeeSpring and RedBubble, but I'm not adding anything to them. It could be a time issue. I don't have the time to put much effort into those avenues.

If all you're doing is shirts, then it may turn out better for you. I must make time for writing, designing, uploading, and my wife and daughter. My daughter gets a good portion of my time, and I wouldn't have it any other way. Fun fact: She's sitting next to me watching YouTube videos while I write this.

One thing you can do while you're waiting to be accepted to Merch by Amazon, or waiting to be tiered up, is to open a few accounts at the places above. Then you can upload your designs and have something selling. It would be a good place to test out your designs. If they sell on TeeSpring and RedBubble, they're going to sell on Amazon. You can have an army of designs waiting for upload.

Educational Resources

This would be going wide with your Ignite products. This will be the shortest section ever. Teacherspayteachers.com is the only one of note. I haven't uploaded there yet, however. It's all still very new to me, and I only have a few products so far. I do plan on uploading there in the next few months. It's one of those things I'll have time for when my daughter is on summer vacation.

Audiobooks

This is another one with very few options. There is Findaway Voices and Author's Republic. I chose Findaway Voices for one very big reason: Author's Republic goes through Findaway Voices. So, I lose a middleman with Findaway.

This is the best option for those who aren't able to use ACX. The narrators are more expensive, however. They do have a new royalty share program now. It's called Voices Share. The good news for those who had their audiobooks created at ACX is, all those files should pass Findaway Voices' quality test. All mine have, including the one I recorded for Dale L Roberts' brother, Walt.

I'll mention his book because I recorded the audiobook, and it is also about making money. It's called Live Streaming Kit$_2$ and you guessed it, Walt shows you how to make money using various live streaming services, including Twitch, Facebook, YouTube, and many more. It's one of those short reads I was telling you about, and it's packed with a lot of useful information. He went wide with the audiobook, so that's available wherever you get your audiobooks.

Findaway Voices will distribute your audiobooks to many places that ACX will not. They'll also get you into libraries. ACX and Findaway Voices both get you into the Apple Store, but Findaway Voices gives you more of the royalty than ACX does. As a bonus, if you uploaded to ACX then Findaway, Apple favors Findaway. So, you won't have to worry about ACX giving you the smaller royalty, you'll be covered by Findaway. Remember, you can't use Findaway Voices (or anyone else) if you're on an exclusive contract with ACX.

Chapter 10 Exercise

Decide where you're going to go next. Look at all your options and create an account there. When you're ready to go wide, you'll be ready to go, no excuses.

CHAPTER 11 STOCK PHOTOGRAPHY AND ILLUSTRATIONS

*S*o here we are, making money online without Amazon. Even though I say the easiest way to make money online is through Amazon, you can still do it elsewhere with good results. And you don't have to sell your soul trying to spam affiliate links or waste your money on scammy solo ads.

No worries, we can begin sentences with "and" now. The Founders did it in the Constitution, Article IV, section 1 – "And the Congress may by general laws..." Awesome, right? English lessons are free here!

So, you don't need to be a professional photographer to upload to stock sites. You don't have to be a professional artist or designer to upload illustrations. I'm one, but not the other. But I upload and sell both. I was a US Navy Photographer and went to Photography School at NAS Pensacola, Florida. Great times. It was considered a top photo school.

That was back in the days of film, and I kind of miss film. I got stationed at the Fleet Intelligence Center Pacific in Pearl Harbor, HI. Don't look for it; it no longer exists. While I was there, all the base closures were happening. Pearl is still there, of course. All the intelligence agencies on the Island combined into one – the Joint Intelligence Center Pacific. Original, right?

It was mostly Navy personnel still, but the Army and Air Force were there too. The Marines were always there with us. It was in Hawaii where I started learning to make money with my camera. I learned about stock photography but didn't get into it much at the time. I was in a major tourist area and took photos of tourists. Then I put them on magazine covers and other things.

Today I have photos on several stock photography sites and on a photo art site. That one pulls in a big chunk of change when one sells – compared to stock photography. That is called Fine Art America.

So you can deduce that I'm not a designer or artist (besides photography.) But after browsing thousands of illustrations and purchasing almost 200 of them, I came to realize that I could make some basic illustrations and sell them on the sites.

The pro is going to sell more than me on any given day. But I still make money. It's all about multiple income streams. The more I have sending me money, the better. If it's only $20, I'll take it. If it's more, awesome! Just diversify and get those streams coming to you. Like anything else, the more designs you put up there, the more money you can make.

This is one you can go wide from right out of the gate. Just remember, a lot of places make you do a little online class and then take a test before you can start uploading. They want you to be aware of the rules, especially trademark rules. You can't have brand names in photographs, and in some cases, you can't have buildings. When drawing, stay away from known characters, like Disney and Marvel, for instance.

There is an exception in photography. If it's art, then it can have brand names. My cigar art is covered in brand names, all on the cigar bands. But I'm covered there. I can't put any of those photos up on the stock sites, however. Well, I *can* but I won't. They will try to sell it as art, but I won't make the money I make at Fine Art America.

Photography

You not only don't need to be a professional, you don't need a professional camera. It helps, of course, but if you've got a good camera on your smartphone, you may have enough. I remember a long time ago, the first iPhone photo was accepted at one of the stock sites. Which one, I'll never remember.

Phone cameras have come a long way since then. Odds are, whatever phone you're using, the camera in it is better than the old iPhone camera. Any DSLR camera is an improvement over a cell phone, however. DSLR is Digital Single Lens Reflex. It's a camera you can change lenses on. I use a Canon 5D Mark III with all prime lenses, half being the awesome L series lenses. The other half, I'd love the L series, but can't afford them. My wife tells me so.

"L" stands for "Luxury," and it kind of makes me laugh. They are the top of the line Canon lenses. I don't suggest going right out and buying L series lenses, however. Buy the mid-grade lenses and stay away from the kit lenses.

Image quality is important on stock sites, and the 5D delivers, especially with quality lenses. The 5D is a full frame camera, meaning it has a large image sensor. Others are called "crop" cameras. They have smaller sensors, and it affects the image quality.

For those of you who remember film cameras, a full frame would be like a 4x5 camera, and the crop would be a 35mm, or even a 110 if the sensor is small enough. The 110 would be your cell phone cameras. You'll have your work cut out for you with a cell phone, but it can be done.

If your camera takes video, that's a bonus. You are able to

upload video to stock photography sites too. They accept HD and 4k. It's a good way to double up your inventory. Even better, you can have video at normal speed, then use a video editor to slow a clip down and have a slow-motion clip too. You upload them as separate files. You'll have two chances to sell the same clip. If you can record in slow motion, do that instead. Film at normal speed, then slow it down. It works well with water, people, and nature. You can speed up cars and get two clips out of them.

What to shoot?

People sell. But there are a few things to consider: 1. You must have anyone in the shot or video sign a model release. The stock sites have them for you to download. 2. No brand names. You must tell your models to dress accordingly. For photos, you can remove a lot of the brand names while editing, but it's best to prevent brands from showing up.

People at work sell the best. If you can get into a doctor's office or exam room, you'll do well. Business offices and meetings sell well too. Other than that, people at play, at the beach, a picnic at the park, people just about anywhere.

While you're at the park, get photos of any fountains you see. If people are in the way, don't let it bother you. If they're facing away from the camera, you can include them. Sometimes it makes the photo better. If a face is unrecognizable, you're good without a model release.

Inanimate objects do well. Try to shoot from unusual angles and see what happens. Things like bikes, playground equipment, boats of all kinds, and more. Try to think differently than your everyday self. Look at things in a different way. See them differently. Shoot in landscape and portrait – horizontal and vertical for the newbies.

You want your photographs to stand out. It helps to browse the stock sites and see what everyone is doing. Then do something different. Study the composition – how the scene is set.

Learn the rule of thirds. This will help you compose your shots. This is something else you can learn on YouTube for free. If you've taken any kind of photography or drawing/painting class, you should already know this rule. The short version is never put your subject in the center of the photo. There is more to it, however.

If you have a person or animal looking left or right, never have the face on the edge they're looking. So, if the person is looking left, the face should be on the right side – looking into the photograph. If you put them on the left side, looking out, you take the viewer's eyes off the photo. You've lost them.

There are a few things you shouldn't shoot: animals and flowers. They are overloaded with both. If you have something unique, go ahead and try it. I took an awesome shot of a tiger in a zoo, and it got accepted. It looks like the tiger is in the wild, walking right at the viewer, licking her lips. If you're confident you have a unique photo, go for it.

Illustrations

This is another place you can shine with your Illustrator or Designer skills – or whatever vector software you're using. Especially if you're an artist. But don't worry, once you learn a few simple skills, you can sell illustrations even if you aren't an artist.

I started with simple smiley faces. As I learned, they got better. Smileys can be made using only the shape tools. Easy peasy. One YouTube channel I recommend is Affinity Revolution - bit.ly/Revolution-YT. It's a husband and wife team, and they make videos for all of Affinity's products. Search their channel, and you'll find videos teaching you how to make various animals.

At the same time, it teaches you how to use a lot of the functions. They also only use the shape tools to create the designs.

If you aren't using Affinity, it still may help you, but I would search for your product and "how to." It will also serve you well to take a few classes on Udemy or elsewhere. Basic design is always a good start.

Not all stock sites will accept illustrations. But that's ok; you'll get enough opportunities. If you're doing shirts and/or journals, you'll know what people are looking for. That gives you an advantage over people just throwing anything up.

If you aren't doing those things, use Amazon to search the top selling journals and t-shirts. You'll see what people are putting on their covers and shirts. That's the kinds of things you'll need to be making. Unlike the photo sites, animals will do well here: from kids' animals to intricate designs. So those animals you learn to make on Affinity Revolution's YouTube channel will do good here. Just remember to make them a little different. I've seen people upload those already.

Some tips: Always use a transparent background. People are putting these into their designs, and a white background isn't going to cut it. The buyer can remove the background, but it takes time.

I will always pass on a design that isn't transparent unless it's the only one. I've seen some intricate designs on a white background and cringed at the amount of work it would take to remove it all. Not. Gonna. Do it. I've also seen multicolored backgrounds, and that's even worse! I can't imagine those sell well. DepositPhotos only sells .jpgs for some reason. It bugs me. So, your transparent background will be white.

Another thing I see is people making logos and adding words. Why? Don't do that. The buyer has their own words they'd like to use. This is something else adding more work for the buyer. The more work you cause the buyer, the less likely a design is to sell. Do you want to write cool words in a fancy new font or get paid? I like getting paid.

Where possible, upload the file in .png, .jpg, and a .svg file (DepositPhotos only accepts .jpg and .eps.) Put them in a zip file and upload them that way. On DepositPhotos, you can download a vector instead of a .jpg, which is what I do when I'm buying designs. I try to make everything, but I'm not an artist, so I still buy designs. I always try the .eps file first, hoping it was made on a transparent background. Most people are awesome and do so. The .eps will also allow me to resize the illustration without losing any quality. That's what vectors do.

So where should you upload all your photos and/or designs? There are quite a few stock sites, some better than others and some offer higher royalties for being exclusive with them. I don't do exclusive, but that's a decision for you to make on your own. Read the benefits and see if it's right for you.

I'm going to stick to the big ones and the ones POD users use. All but one of the following accept photos, video, and illustrations (vectors mostly.) Shutterstock.com, istockphoto.com, fotolia.com, gettyimages.com, bigstockphoto.com, depositphotos.com, and creativefabrica.com. There are many more, but that's a good start. If you want more, just search "stock sites," and you will be inundated with places to upload your work.

DepositPhotos and Creative Fabrica are the two that POD users use most. Creative Fabrica does not accept photos or video. You'll have to browse their site to get a feel for what they're offering. But if you know how to create fonts, they do accept font uploads.

Chapter 11 Exercises

Ok, it's homework time again! I can hear you screaming,

"Woohoo!" Maybe you're just screaming. But it's good for you. Taking action will separate you from almost everyone else.

This one can be fun! Either grab your camera and take some awesome photographs and/or video or create a design or two. If you already have designs, you're ahead of the game. Cool! Then you need to create an account on at least one of the sites above, and when you're able, upload your work. Work you can enjoy is awesome work!

CHAPTER 12 EMAIL MARKETING

I just heard you deflate. Ok, this isn't the most fun thing to do, but it's a huge advantage for everything in the KDP chapter and audiobooks. You don't have to do this, but it will increase your profit and reduce your marketing costs. When getting started, you don't even need to pay for an email service.

So, why do you need email marketing? Every time you write a new book, you get to send out an email to let everyone know about it. That will send a surge of buyers to Amazon, increasing your rank. With your rank up there, more people will see your book and some of them will purchase it – keeping your rank up there.

A lot of authors also do newsletters, keeping people up to date every week, two weeks, or once a month. I do not do that, but I should. With a newsletter, you can do newsletter swaps with others *in your genre*. Don't go outside your genre; you'll lose subscribers. If you're writing clean contemporary romance, don't swap with someone writing anything else. "Clean" means no swearing, no sex, etc. Squeaky clean.

A note on being clean: You'll get more sales. A lot of people don't want to see swearing or sex in the books they read. Parents buy books for their kids, and they're looking for "clean." Believe it or not, clean romance is huge. If you're writing clean, make sure your emails reflect that. Don't go on a profanity-laced rant in an email. It won't go over well.

Back to newsletters. A newsletter swap is not a review swap and is perfectly fine to do. You can find other authors to swap with in Facebook groups and at storyoriginapp.com. Story Origin is a free service at the time I'm writing this, and it's pretty awesome. This is where you can set up newsletter swaps. If you have a free book to give away for people to sign up to your list, you can upload it, and Story Origin will give you a link to share and integrate with some email services. If there isn't integration, you can download the signups and upload them to your service.

Evan Gow is the owner, and he's a nice guy. He must be; he's offering all this for free! For now. He will be charging at some point, so get there asap.

A swap is simple. You agree with another author or authors to email your list on an agreed upon date. You will inform your list about said author's book and give a link to where they can purchase it. That author will also email his or her list on a date you choose.

It accomplishes a few things; you get more sales, and those sales turn into more subscribers. Unfortunately, not everyone who buys your book will sign up for your list – especially if you don't have something to offer them in return. But that's ok, subscribers will come.

So how do you get your subscribers?

It ain't easy. But nothing worthwhile is. First, you need a service. I recommend Mailchimp when you're first starting out. It's free for your first 2000 subscribers, which is pretty cool. It will probably take you a while to reach 2000. I never had Mailchimp so I can't give any advice on it. But just about every author I know either used it or is currently using it. They say good things.

I use Active Campaign, and I'll tell you, it has a steep learning curve. There is also Aweber, GetResponse, and Constant Contact, to name a few. But those all charge right out of the gate. I don't see a reason to use them when you're new. I wish I knew about Mailchimp when I started. It would have saved me a lot of money.

So, after you've signed up for your service, you'll need to decide if you'll be offering a freebie to entice (bribe) people to sign up for your list. Doing so will build your list faster. Not offering a freebie will populate your list with fewer people, but they'll be bigger fans because they signed up without getting anything in return.

What can you offer? It depends on what you've written. For fiction, you should offer a short story that is connected to your book. You can create a story in your book but not tell it! You hint at it, make it a memory that doesn't get fully explained. Then you tell the story in the short story. You've created curiosity in the book, so more people will want to sign up to read it.

For nonfiction, you can get creative. You can offer a short report on the topic of your book; you can offer a free training, or just about anything else, so long as it can be delivered via email. You can get a Dropbox account to host your giveaway and provide a link to it.

I use Product Dyno to host all my giveaway items - kevinbarrymaguire.com/Product-Dyno. It's fast, secure, and integrates with most autoresponder services. So, when someone signs up for your list, they do so on a Product Dyno page, then their information is sent to your email service while the reader is sent to your download page. You can host documents, photographs, audio, and video, any digital products, really. Using Product Dyno prevents people from taking your products without giving an email address.

Let's say you wrote a small book about manifesting so you can sell a product from Clickbank. You can offer a free report on manifesting if they sign up for your list. Be sure to check the offer page to see if they offer reports for you. If they do, make sure you edit the report to insert your affiliate link into the report. Don't do what I did and send free traffic somewhere. I still cringe thinking about that.

Maybe you wrote, or had a ghostwriter write, a book about mindful meditation. Then you got your creative juices flowing and recorded a guided meditation as your freebie. Nothing says you have to offer a document. You can even create a video and either put it on YouTube set to private, or upload it to Product Dyno.

The more creative you get, the more people will sign up for your list. Reports are a dime a dozen, keep that in mind. I read a few weeks ago that people are getting tired of reports. So be creative. Put some thought into your offer and make sure you deliver *value*. If you need to put money into it, do it. It will be worth it in the long run.

Now what?

Now that you have your offer, if you're offering one, you need to put it somewhere. Put it where the sun does shine! Right in your book. I know you've seen this done before, and you'll see it at the end of this book. It's the most effective place to put the offer.

Most people put it at the end of the book; some put it at the beginning and the end. I think I tried that once but changed my mind on it and only put it at the end now. I think it reeks of desperation to have it at the start. The readers don't even know you yet; why would they sign up to your list? Keep it at the end.

You can say, "If you'd like to get my free doohickey about

basket weaving, be sure to sign up for my email list at free-doohickey@basketsrock.com. I know you'll enjoy it."

Any variation of that will work. At this point, you've already thanked them for purchasing your book. *You did thank them, right?* Of course, you did. Never forget to thank the readers; it's bad mojo. It should be the first thing you do at the end of the book. Without them, you won't get anywhere.

After that you can put your email offer. If you have other books, you can list those next. Provide links to make it easy for the reader. If you have an Amazon Associates account, do not put Amazon affiliate links in the book – eBook and paperback. Amazon does not allow it.

I suggest applying for an Associates account. You can put the links anywhere else, just not in books you upload to Amazon. When you go wide, you can replace the clean Amazon links with your affiliate links. So, if you bought this book on Amazon, you can be sure all Amazon links are not affiliate links.

If you have a website, you can ask people to sign up for your list from there, before they even read the book. If your website is informative and gives value, people will sign up. You can get them to your books via email, once they've signed up.

If you have the money to spend, you can run ads to your free offer and get subscribers that way. Make sure you have a quality offer before going that route, however. You'll need good ad copy to go with it too. You don't want to be wasting money on clicks that don't produce subscribers. I've never gone this route, but I know Jacob Rothenberg has.

I know you've probably signed up for many lists already, so you should know what to do. Your first email to your new subscribers should be a welcome email. Thank them for signing up and let them know what to expect. Give any contact information you feel comfortable with and leave a list of your books for sale.

Don't give out your phone number. Emails and websites are

fine. I have four websites and email for two of them, so for me, I'll put, "Contact me via email at kevin@kevinbarrymaguire.com" and my website. That's all you really need to put in there. Try not to write long emails. If you become known for telling your life story in every email, people will stop opening them.

After that, you want to write a few informative emails. Again, give value. Do not sell anything in those emails. After you've written two or three value emails, you can pitch a product or service in the next one. Rinse, repeat. Just like long emails, people don't want to get bombarded with offers.

I'm on a list from a person who can't stop with the offers. The person will give a good tip but always follow with an offer related to the tip. I like the person, but I stopped reading the emails. I may open 25% of them now. If you take care of your subscribers, they'll take care of you. I read something from Ava Fails about a good way to keep subscribers happy – offer some freebies along the way. Not too many, but a few a year. Contests work wonders too. You can offer an Amazon gift card to the winner or winners. Creativity wins.

Besides your autoresponder series, you can send out periodic emails. Again, most with useful information and some with offers. Don't be the one who's quiet for two months, then pops in with an offer, only to disappear again for a few months. How often depends on you and your schedule.

Some do weekly emails, and I don't see where they get the time. I know a few of them, and I know how busy they are. Some are bi-weekly, and others are monthly. I know one guy who only emails twice a year. I wouldn't go that far, however. He's kind of a big deal, and people wait for those emails.

A lot of people don't like the idea of email marketing; it's more of a fear. Don't be like them. Email marketing is a great way to market your books and any offers you may find. There is no other way that is better, especially for the price. Sending emails is free, advertising is not.

. . .

Chapter 12 Exercise

I think you know what's coming... besides massive action. Head on over to Mailchimp and sign up for an account. Why Mailchimp? Because it's free, and you won't waste money waiting for those first subscribers. But you will have your account ready and waiting.

CHAPTER 13 IGNITE

This will be a short chapter. Even though at least six weeks have passed since I wrote the first chapter, Ignite is still very new. I have uploaded some projects, but so far, I have zero sales. I'm not alone. Very few people have had sales so far. The two Facebook groups I'm in have become very quiet. The consensus is, Amazon is waiting until they have enough material before they start promoting the service to customers. So, we must keep uploading.

Some people use Amazon to do their research. I use Teachers Pay Teachers, simply because there is more there, for now. Also, because there are very few sales for Ignite products on Amazon, there are no BSR rankings. We don't know what's going to sell and what isn't.

Over at Teachers Pay Teachers (TPT), we can see how many reviews a product has, along with the overall star rating. If you're going to use Amazon, switch the search dropdown from "all" to "digital educational resources."

There is a great search function at TPT: you can zero in on grade level, higher education, adult education, and homeschool.

And you can browse by grade level, subject, price, and resource type. On the bottom left of the page, you can browse a lot of resource types. Doing that will give you a lot of ideas for your own projects.

Once again, don't copy anyone's projects. Use them for inspiration. A lot of people at TPT signed up for Ignite and have uploaded all their stuff there too. Copycats will be found with ease, since the number of projects on Ignite is relatively small.

If you're uncomfortable making educational products, you can make posters, clip art, games, flash cards, and more. If you have kids in school, go to the classrooms and see what's hanging on the walls. That is what you can make. If you don't, ask a friend or family member to let you tag along to a class sometime. Don't go unaccompanied if you don't have kids in school. You may be accused of being a little creepy. You must check in at the office, and they may not believe your reason.

I've been using Affinity Publisher to create my products. If I need to create illustrations, shapes, or any vectors, I can switch to Designer from inside Publisher and do what I need to do, then switch back to Publisher with ease. It's one of the best features Affinity has that Adobe does not. I make the cover in Designer. Yep, you need a cover. The product can be uploaded in many formats: .doc, .docx, .pdf, .xls, .xlsx, .ppt, .pptx, .jpg, .png, .txt, and .zip. The cover may only be either .jpg or .png.

If you want to know what the cover should look like, just head over to TPT and look at the listings. The image you see is the cover. It shows what the person is getting and can include text information. For all the specs and other help, be sure to read the help page, https://ignite.amazon.com/edu/#/help.

When you log into Ignite, you see the upload section and "My resources." You can drag and drop or browse to upload. First, you'll upload your product, then your cover. It will also ask if you have a preview to upload. I don't do that. Amazon will create one for you if you don't. It's like the "Look Inside" feature for books on Amazon. Then you wait. And wait. The review process is long.

Unfortunately, Ignite doesn't have the fancy Reports page that KDP has. There is a Repost tap on the top left of the page, click it. Then choose a date range. It will take a few seconds, then the "Download Report" button will become active. Download it, then open it. It's a lot of trouble to see zero sales. But guess what? I went through it to make sure I didn't miss anything and holy moly, I got a sale! So, I've made my first $2 on Ignite. I'm sure there will be much more to come.

Unfortunately, this is all there is to it at the moment. But if you sign up to my email list, I'll keep you informed of any updates and any new stuff I've learned. I won't be holding back any advice. If I know it, you'll know it.

My friend, Keith Wheeler, has a great YouTube channel for low-content books and has been doing Ignite videos too. I suggest you check him out. He goes through the research process and the upload process. bit.ly/Keith-YT

Chapter 13 Exercise

Ok, whether you've been accepted to Ignite or not, you should do this exercise. When you are accepted, you will have something ready to upload. If you aren't accepted, you will still be able to use Teachers Pay Teachers.

Head over to Teachers Pay Teachers and browse around. Look for something you'd like to create and make sure there are a lot of reviews in the niche. Then get to creating! Design a product you're proud of and edit it to make sure everything is right. Remember, kids are counting on you to get it right. So are the teachers.

Upload if you're able, put it in a folder for later if you can't upload yet.

AFTERWORD

"Someone out there is holding their breath waiting for you to fail. Make sure they suffocate." I saw that meme on Facebook, and it's true. If you take action and use the exercises I give you, those who wish you to fail *will* suffocate. Hopefully, you did them all, and the next one. Wait... what? Next one? More homework? You bet. The Final.

You now have the tools to start your online business; only you can stop you now. You can start most of these options with little or no money, so get started. Don't let anything stand in your way. Working online has distractions – Facebook, Twitter, and the rest of the Internet. Don't let them sidetrack you. Block out time for those activities.

Pay attention to my examples. I used good keywords for you to take advantage of. Take the hint and run with it. Keyword research will be the hardest part of the process when you're starting out; use what I gave you and make it easier.

Speaking of keywords, while you're on Facebook and Twitter, pay attention to the memes. Don't just laugh at them, study them. Figure out which one will take off before everyone else does and make a t-shirt or journal cover with it. I've made some good money using that tactic. Do not make a "meme book," however.

Someone in a Facebook group did that and was making a lot of sales, until Amazon smacked him down for it. He used the actual photos from the memes, photos he didn't have the rights to use. When creating your designs, use the text, not the photos. You can use stock images, if you choose to use any.

Once you master the keyword research, you'll be on your way to better times. Lucky for you, it doesn't take long to master. When you find that awesome keyword that nobody else found, you'll feel like you're walking on air. Then you're going to get very excited. I found one for a nonfiction book once, only one person had a book in the keyword, and it was a keyword Amazon suggested early. I couldn't believe it. The book I have in that keyword has made me a lot of money, the audiobook too.

It took me several days of hard searching to find that keyword. I don't know how many searches I ran before I tripped over it, but it was all worth it. I'm much better at it now, and I have Publisher Rocket - kevinbarrymaguire.com/Publisher-Rocket. Experience and the right software make it all go faster.

The Final Exercise

This is where all the action you took earlier in the book comes together. You've done the research. You've got your keywords and pain points. You know what people want more of and what they don't like. Write the book. One more Dale-ism (even though he says he didn't make it up) – Done is better than perfect. Write it, edit it, publish it. You can use a ghostwriter too.

If you have no interest in writing, no worries. You have other options. Choose any of the other ways to make money from this book and get it done. Make 100 t-shirt designs. Create 100 vectors. Audition for audiobook narration jobs. Design 100 educational products. Get 50 photographs approved on a stock site.

I gave you the tools to make the money, but only you can take the action required. The more you put into this, the more you're going to get out of it. You can take it slow and make a little money, or you can bust through the gate and keep running like Bo Jackson screaming out of the Kingdome. But you must take action. That is a serious cliché, I know. But it's also true. You can do this.

I'm going to leave you with a final quote from Ava Fails, it came from one of her emails. You can find her at HeyYoAva.com.

Making money online is a long game.

There's nothing easy here. There's no button to push.

It's all roll up your sleeves and start digging dirty work. Get in shape because we chase EVERY dollar.

THANKS!

Thanks for making it through to the end of The Real Way to Make Money Online, let's hope it was informative and able to provide you with all of the tools you need to achieve your financial goals, whatever it is that they may be. Just because you've finished this book doesn't mean there is nothing left to learn on the topics, and expanding your horizons is the only way to find the long-term success you seek.

Now that you have finished this book you are no doubt chomping at the bit to get ready to get started with one, or a few, of the avenues mentioned. It is important to take the advice in the previous chapters seriously, however, and give yourself plenty of time to learn and make money in one before starting another. The exception being Merch, because it's a slow roll at the start. By all means, start Merch as soon as you're able – along with whichever other option you chose first.

Finally, if you found this book useful in anyway, a review on Amazon is always appreciated, you can go here to leave a review: bit.ly/MakeMoney-Review

Thanks again!

You can reach me from my website – kevinbarrymaguire.com or you can sign up for my email list for some free goodies at https://kevinbarrymaguire.com/POD-Signup. I've got some templates made to get you started in no and low-content publishing. I'll also keep you up to date with everything new happening in the print on demand world – including everything about Ignite! Pay attention because I will periodically offer more free goodies to those on my list.

I offer one-on-one coaching via Skype for anyone who needs help on anything discussed in this book. Email me at: kevin@kevinbarrymaguire.com to learn more.

THE EXPERTS

Throughout this book, you've seen a lot of tips from the experts. I've been lucky enough to know all these people and call several of them a friend. While I'm very good at some things, nobody can be an expert at everything. So it was great to be able to have these people lend some expert advice.

Now I'm going to introduce them to you and let you know where to reach them. They all have YouTube channels, so that's cool.

Dale L Roberts

I'll start with the man who got me started in all this. If it weren't for him, I'd have never written my first book and it never would have been a best seller. I'd have never knocked John Grisham out of the #1 spots. I owe that all to Dale.

Dale is a wealth of knowledge in the self-publishing arena. Some call him an encyclopedia on self-publishing. They're right. I started watching his videos on YouTube when I was still trying to scrape by with affiliate marketing, and spending a lot of money on crap that didn't work.

Then Dale offered his course and I thought I'd give it a try. In that course, I won individual and group coaching with Dale. The rest, as they say, is history. In the group coaching, Dale challenged us to write a short story, and that's where Aftermath of Disaster was born.

Today I call Dale a friend and you can sign up for his free course here - kevinbarrymaguire.com/Dales-Startup. It will get you started in self-publishing. You'll learn how to upload and other essentials. You can check out his YouTube channel here, for all kinds of valuable information - bit.ly/Dale-YT. If Twitch is your thing, you can watch Dale live every Monday afternoon - twitch.tv/selfpublish.

Dale has a great course that is constantly updated. There are several price levels, after the free course, so if you choose to take his course, you can choose how deep you want to go.

Kelli "Publish" Roberts

You may think her last name looks familiar, you're right. Kelli and Dale are married and make a great team. Her expertise is in no and low-content books, with a splash of Merch by Amazon. I met her through Dale, of course.

Kelly has mastered her low-content publishing and is a great teacher. As mentioned way back in chapter 4, she made $18k in one month. December. The awesome month. She started appearing in live shows with Dale, then started her own channel and is a super star! Her Tuesday afternoon (12pm Eastern) live shows are popping. If you're going to be doing low and no-content books, that's the place to be. On YouTube, she's Kelli Publish. If you're lucky, their cat Izzy will be sunning herself behind Kelli while she's live. youtube.com/kellipublish

Julie Broad

Julie is another person with vast knowledge of self-publishing. She is the owner of Book Launchers and helps authors write, publish, and promote their books. This is an all in one service for *nonfiction* books only. She has ghost-writers on staff if you want them to do the writing as well. Her bona fides include having the

#1 book on all of Amazon. Not just in a category – *the overall #1 book*. The top 100, she's the top. The tip of the spear.

Julie's videos are informative and fun. You cannot finish one of her videos and not be in a better mood than when you started. I still remember the first video I saw from her and she said, "I'm Julie Broad, the book Broad..." I laughed, because I can get along with anyone who can run with that name. I subscribed on the spot and haven't regretted it.

Most of the people she helps use their books as a tool to other things – speaking gigs, courses, etc. If that is your goal, you can contact her at Book Launchers.com. You can catch her on YouTube here. Just watch one video and you'll understand why I don't miss a single one. You may even win a coffee mug or an oh so soft journal to write in. I have both, they're great! youtube.com/booklaunchers

Jacob Rothenberg

Jacob got my attention the first time I saw him on YouTube. It was on someone else's channel – a guy I won't name because he teaches black hat tactics. Jacob is a master at finding nonfiction keywords and built up a very profitable publishing business from it.

Jacob has also started publishing romance books and is killing it there. He's mastered nonfiction and fiction. He has a course called, The Publishing Evolution – Ultimate Edition - kevinbarrymaguire.com/Publishing-Evolution - and a course for those who have published books already – Revalavi. Don't get Revalavi until you have two to three books in the same niche and have had some success. It's an advanced course - kevinbarrymaguire.com/Revalavi. Of course, Jacob also has a YouTube channel full of informative and entertaining videos. bit.ly/Jacob-YT

Jacob is a funny guy and easy to get along with. What he teaches is the right way to do things. You won't have to worry about losing your account by following what he teaches.

Keith Wheeler

Keith was in Dale's group coaching with me and that's how we met. He writes children's books. He successfully got his books into bookstores as a self-published author – without using an aggregator. That's impressive, trust me. He shows you how to do it on his YouTube channel. After that feat, he was signed on by a traditional publisher.

Keith also does low-content publishing and his YouTube channel is full of great tips. He even has some videos about Ignite. There is only one other person I know of doing Ignite videos, so this is a good place to be! bit.ly/Keith-YT

Paddy aka StackinProfit

Paddy built an impressive business in a short amount of time and has a YouTube channel full of informative videos. He's on a ferocious upload schedule, I don't know where he finds the time. Paddy is another low-content master. He's making a few grand a month doing this as a relative newcomer.

If you really want to see how he does his magic, I strongly recommend his courses - kevinbarrymaguire.com/stackin-profit. He has creative ways of doing keyword research and how to stay organized. I learned a lot from him and best of all, I keep learning because in The Vault, we get a new training video each week. Very few people keep their courses updated, I don't think anyone else does it weekly. bit.ly/Stackin-Profit

LINKS DISCUSSED IN THIS BOOK

Dale L Robert Course:

https://kevinbarrymaguire.com/Dales-Startup

https://kevinbarrymaguire.com/Dales-Basic

His YouTube Channel:

https://bit.ly/Dale-YT

The Kindlepreneur (AKA Dave Chesson)

Publisher Rocket:

https://kevinbarrymaguire.com/Publisher-Rocket

Free Amazon Ads Course:

https://kevinbarrymaguire.com/AMS-Course

7 Kindle Keywords Article

https://kevinbarrymaguire.com/7-Kindle-Keywords

How to Choose Categories:

https://kevinbarrymaguire.com/Choose-Categories

Vellum:

https://kevinbarrymaguire.com/Vellum

Low Content Domination:

https://kevinbarrymaguire.com/Low-Content

Jacob Rothenberg

The Publishing Evolution:
https://kevinbarrymaguire.com/Publishing-Evolution
Revalavi:
https://kevinbarrymaguire.com/Revalavi
Pretty Merch:
https://kevinbarrymaguire.com/Pretty-Merch

StackinProfits

Printin Profits:
https://kevinbarrymaguire.com/Printin-Profits
LCB Vault:
https://kevinbarrymaguire.com/LCB-Vault
Udemy (1000's of courses)
https://kevinbarrymaguire.com/Udemy
Creative Fabrica:
https://kevinbarrymaguire.com/creative-fabrica
Deposit Photos
https://kevinbarrymaguire.com/deposit-photos
Simple Maze Crazy
https://kevinbarrymaguire.com/Maze-Crazy

Book Launchers

http://www.booklaunchers.com/
Book Launchers YouTube
http://www.booklaunchers.com/
Merch Money Masters – Code Kevin
https://kevinbarrymaguire.com/Merch-Money
Arun's Clickbank 2020 Reviews
https://kevinbarrymaguire.com/Clickbank-2020
Steve's Clickbank Review Videos
https://kevinbarrymaguire.com/CB-Videos
Product Dyno
https://kevinbarrymaguire.com/Product-Dyno
Scrivener
https://kevinbarrymaguire.com/Scrivener

Affiliate Notice:

Some of the links in the book are affiliate links and I will get a small kickback for referring you – it comes at no cost to you and in some cases, you save money by using my link. In all cases, you help feed my daughter and her cat.

www.ingramcontent.com/pod-product-compliance
Lightning Source LLC
LaVergne TN
LVHW042335060326
832902LV00006B/174